C000098372

Kingdom of Angels

Dec 21st 2021

Best Wishes,

Love,

Kingdom of Angels

MICHELLE KEANE

Copyright Michelle Keane 2021

The right of Michelle Keane to be identified as the Author of
the Work has been asserted by her in accordance with the
Copyright, Designs and Patents Act 1998.

First published in Ireland in 2021
by Michelle Keane

All rights reserved. No part of this publication may be reproduced, stored in
a retrieval system, or transmitted, in any form or by any means without the
prior written permission of the publisher, nor be otherwise circulated in any
form of binding or cover other than that in which it is published and without
a similar condition being imposed on the subsequent purchaser.

Hardback ISBN 978-1-913698-97-3
Paperback ISBN 978-1-913698-98-0

www.kingdomwater.ie
info@kingdomwater.ie

Cover design by Anú Design, Tara
(www.anu-design.ie)

Typesetting by Inspire.ie

Printed and bound in Castleisland, Co.Kerry by WALSH COLOUR Print
(www.walshcolourprint.com)

Kingdom Water logo designed by aidan@avalanchedesigns.ie

KINGDOM
WATER

To Luke & Holly
A pair of grounded angels

Contents

Preface

This is my second book. The follow-up to *The Discovery of Kingdom Water*, published in 2020.

That story started in May 2018, with a bottle of water filled from St Michael's Well in Ballinskelligs, County Kerry, Ireland, and a vision I saw of St Patrick. I knew then that something very strange was happening me, but I've always been a very spiritual and religious person, and so I simply accepted it. I don't know why I felt like that, it just felt natural within my soul.

I knew that my life was going to change. And it did.

Through Divine and angelic signs and assistance, I found seven natural underground springs on my land. This became Kingdom Water, and the journey to create a business from that became the subject of my first book.

Throughout that journey, the angel interventions and spiritual signs became more intense. As I learned from and about these signs, I knew I wanted to write a second book, and that this book would be dedicated to understanding more about these angels, and the way they had come into my life.

I followed a path that was laid out for me, on which I was guided every step of the way by my ancestors and the angels who came to me in visions. I travelled far and wide – to India, France, Italy, Portugal and throughout Ireland, and learned about the meaning of angels in many societies, religions and cultures. I began to understand the ways in which God moves his angels as messengers and comforters.

I have brought together everything that I learned on this quest in this book, Kingdom of Angels, because I want to show you that angels are in our midst all the time, if only we choose to pay attention to them. This book will teach you how to recognise angels in your life, how to reach out to them, communicate with them and interpret what they tell you.

I don't know why any of this happened to me. I have asked myself this question many times along the way, and part of me always will ask. But eventually I have had to stop questioning, and just accept that I was intended, by Our Lady and the angels, to write this book.

The book you now hold in your hands is my honouring of these Divine instructions. It is the result of an angelic directive, and provides a nondenominational overview of who the angels are; their role in various spiritual texts and religions; the way angels help us and how we can call upon them; information on guardian angels and archangels and frequently asked questions about the angels.

This book will teach you to recognise angels and divine messengers in your own life. It will show you how to reach out to them, communicate with them and interpret what they say. God communicates with all of us, all the time, and in *Kingdom of Angels* I want to show you the clear and easily-followed steps that enable all of us to connect with our own angels.

Chapter 1

Who Are Angels?

I have always been fascinated by angels. I can still vividly remember my mother, Thérèse, shouting from the bottom of the staircase on Monday morning the 1ˢᵗ September 1980, *"Get up Michelle or you will be late for your first day at school"*. I wanted to wake up, but I felt scared too. I was nervous of what my first day of school would bring.

The first day of school is full of change. Summer is over and waking up early is about to become the new norm for a five-year-old. It's a new level of transition. I had no expectation of what my first day at school would bring. When I arrived home, my mother asked me *"well, how was your first day at school?"*, I said *"mam I sat next to an angel and her name was Ella"*.

Ella was indeed an angel. She developed leukaemia and died at the age of six-and-a-half. Her death had a profound effect on me, and I still visit her grave 40 years later.

I remember back and I can still visualise Ella. She looked and walked like an angel, and had a heart of gold. Her smile was precious like a jewel on a crown, her eyes were so deep you could drown in them. She was as pure as the morning dew. But the ones blessed with her charm in this world are few; she was as divine as an angel, without any doubt.

Angels are created by God. Everything in heaven and on earth, both seen and unseen, was created by God for His purpose. There are thousands of angels. We know a few of them by name from the Bible stories, but truth be told there are far more angels than we can probably comprehend. Regardless of their mission, they all report to God. Many of the angels we know by name were messengers. They appeared to men and women of God in order to share a specific message for him. But not all angels are messengers. Some fight wars, others protect and some bring about God's judgement. But no matter what purpose an angel is assigned, they are given that assignment by God, and they carry out his plans and purposes.

Most religious traditions include a form of angel that performs the basic function of advising people that they are in the presence of the Divine. Angels are seen throughout the Old and New Testaments: God sent the Angel Gabriel to Nazareth with a message for Mary, who was promised in marriage to Joseph.

The Angel told Mary that she would have a son, whom she was to name Jesus. The Angel said, "he will be great and will be called the son of the Highest God". Mary asked how this could be as she was a virgin. The Angel Gabriel answered, "The Holy Spirit will come on you, and God's power will rest on you". Mary accepted what God wanted. She was taking a great risk, she knew. She would probably have to take public shame and perhaps Joseph would be angry, yet Mary did not doubt the Angel's message, and gave her acceptance.

The Bhagavad Gita is Hinduism's main sacred text. While Hinduism does not feature angels in the sense that Judaism, Christianity and Islam do, Hinduism does include a myriad of spiritual beings who act in angelic ways. In Hinduism such angelic beings include major gods like Lord Krisha, the Bhagavad Gita author. Hindus respect Lord Krisha as a reincarnation of Lord Vishnu who is one of the principal deities of Hinduism. Vishnu is part of the Hindu Trinity that includes Brahma and Shiva:

GOD
G – God the Father, General Brahma Creator
O – God the Son, Operator Lord Vishnu, The Redeemer
D – God the Holy Spirit, Destroyer Lord Shiva, Bringer of Change and Destruction

Whenever the world is threatened with evil, chaos and destructive forces, Vishnu descends in the form of an avatar (incarnation) to restore the cosmic order and protect Dharma. In the Mahabharata, Vishnu states to Naranda that he will appear in ten incarnations, appearing in the form of a swan, a tortoise, a fish, a boar, a half-man-half lion, and a dwarf, among others.

Hindus believe any human being can rise to the angel status on full self-realisation and payback of all his Karmic debts. They are then considered and accepted as celestial beings in the service of God as assisting entities who have no Karma bonds or rebirth obligations.

Similarly, Hindus believe Buddha is the reincarnation of Lord Vishnu.

Buddhists believe in many of the different types of celestial and semi-divine beings that populate Hindu myth.

The classic angelic function of guardianship and protection resides in other classes of beings who are regarded as Gods in some sects. Many Buddhist temples depict these beings as muscular, heavily-armed gatekeepers. They believe there is a personal deity assigned to each individual, and these protectors can take on either benevolent or angry form, depending on whether they are dealing with a believer or with an enemy of faith.

Despite your religion, it does not matter whether you are Buddhist, Christian, Muslin or Hindu or whether you practice religion at all. What matters is your feeling of oneness with humankind.

Angels are found in the scriptures of all the world's religions and mythologies, and images of these gracious winged comforters abound in the art of every great culture, from the massive winged beasts of stone in ancient Egypt, to the delicate miniatures of the renaissance.

The Old Testament features about 300 stories of angels. Christianity took them over, developing an elaborate love of angels. The Renaissance period produced the greatest flowering of angelic art, when thousands of exquisitely beautiful images graced the paintings of Leonardo da Vinci, Michelangelo, Raphael and Donatella, all famous for their masterworks. The stained-glass windows and frescoes of many Renaissance churches depict beautiful interpretations of angelic beings.

In the 18th century, Swedish scientist and philosopher Emanuel Swedenborg spent over 20 years exploring angels and the spiritual world in his writings. He describes things he saw in heaven, including conversations he had with angels there. While some traditions like to see angels as a supernatural class of beings, Swedenborg declares that every angel was once a human being living on earth.

Based on his experiences, he believes with full confidence that in their form, angels are completely human. They have faces, eyes, ears, chests, arms, hands and feet. They can see each other, hear each other and talk to each other. In short, they lack nothing that belongs to humans except that they are not clothed with a material body.

His belief was that all people on earth have the potential to become angels, regardless of where they are from or what religion they practice. Swedenborg emphasises that we are all born from heaven. If we do not end up there, it is because of the choices that we make in life.

Angels are a bridge between truth and the unhappy experience of problems. They can bring you back from that horror into your happy waking state of health, happiness, peace and abundance. They work in conjunction with your higher self and the soul you are spiritually aligned with, such as Jesus, Mother Mary, Quan Yin, the Holy Spirit, Buddha, Lord Hanuman, Yogananda, Neem Karoli Baba or whomever.

The angels do not judge your beliefs. Rather they work within your present thoughts as a way to reach you. When people shed their physical bodies and enter the spiritual world, at first, they look much the same as they did on earth. Over time however, their inner selves are revealed, and this changes the way they appear to others.

The closer angels get to God, the more beautiful they become. Angels may have halos or wings. Angels of the higher heavens might appear to be dressed in radiant light because bright light corresponds to wisdom.

Angels look youthful. This is because people in heaven are continually progressing towards the springtime of life. They lead busy lives that may not seem that different from ours. They live in houses with all the usual sorts of rooms and their communities are organised very much like towns and cities, with streets and parks and other central buildings.

Communities in heaven are distinguished by the type of service they provide. For example, some communities may be dedicated to raising children who have crossed over, while other communities may be focused on serving people who are being awakened from death.

In general, angels perform the specific service for which they are best suited, and this work is one of their greatest joys. Angels like to work with pure people on earth. While angels love the work they do, they are not doing it for their own sake. They are doing it out of a love of being useful and serving others. The Lord works through angels. Everything comes from the Lord.

Angels speak in a language that is similar to ours and it can be spoken or written down. Angels speech comes from their inner core. Angels can tell everything about another person by hearing only a few words. When angels communicate with us, they seem to speak in our native language.

We are all born from heaven, and all children who leave this world are immediately taken up to heaven and become angels. When children first arrive in heaven, they look just as they did on earth. Babies are still babies; children still appear to be the same age they were when they crossed over. They are raised by angels who particularly love children, and who enjoy teaching them spiritual truth.

When these children reach adulthood, they are welcomed into the angelic communities that perfectly correspond to the innate gifts, talents and capacities of the children. Later on, when family members cross over, the children of those families are reunited with them. Though if they have different natures, they will ultimately end up living in different spiritual communities. This, however is not a sadness but a joy, for all must eventually find a place where they are most at home and where their innate gifts can find fullest expression.

All angels have a perfect match. we could think of it as a "Soulmate". If the two do not meet on earth, they will find each other in heaven. When people who were married on earth meet again in the afterlife, if they were truly of one mind, their marriage will continue in heaven. However, if the two people were not truly compatible, they will gradually separate of their own accord.

Throughout heaven, people who are similar gather together and people who are dissimilar part company. This simply means that every community consists of like-minded people. Like are drawn toward like, not by their own will but by the Lord. By birth, we are all gifted with the ability to discern what is true, even to that deepest level where angels are.

Angels bring comfort and reassurance to us all. God has given us free will and your angels will not overstep this. By asking your angels for help, you allow them to help you. Your angels are always by your side, you are continually loved by them and they help you whenever you ask. You are supported by many angels, now and always.

Although your angels will never interfere with your free will, they are poised to help you at every moment. All you need to do is ask. You are never alone in your time of need. They can see solutions to every problem. Listen in stillness for your angel's guidance, which comes upon wings to your heart, mind and body. Their messages always speak of love. Your angels love you unconditionally and eternally.

In the fourth discourse of the Bhagavad Gita, Lord Vishnu says *"Many and various sacrifices are thus spread out before Brahman, known thou that all these are born of action, and thus knowing thou shalt be free. Better than the sacrifice of any objects is the sacrifice of wisdom. O Parantapa all actions in their entirety, O Partha, culminate in wisdom".*

If I speak in the tongues of men or of angels, but do not have love, I am a noisy gong or a clanging cymbal. And if I have prophetic powers and understand all my mysteries and all knowledge, and if I have all faith, so as to remove mountains, but have no love, I am nothing. If I give all I have and if I deliver up my body to be burned, but have no love, I gain nothing.

Love is patient and kind; love does not envy or boast; it is not arrogant or rude. It does not insist on its own way, it is not irritable or resentful; it does not rejoice at wrongdoing, but rejoices with truth. Love bears all things, believes all things, hopes all things, endures all things. Love never ends. As for prophecies, they will pass away; as for tongues, they will cease; as for knowledge it will pass away. For we know in part and we prophesy in part, but when the perfect comes, the partial will pass away. When I was a child, I spoke like a child, I thought like a child, I reasoned like a child. When I became a man, I gave up childish ways. For now we see in a mirror dimly, but then face-to-face. Now I know in part; then I shall know fully, even as I have been fully known.

So now faith, hope, and love abide, these three; but the greatest of these is love.

Corinthians 13 (ESV)

Guardian Angels Prayer

No evil shall befall you
Nor shall affliction come near your tent,
for to His Angels
God has given his Command about you,
that they guard you in all your ways.

*Upon their hands
they will bear you up,
lest you dash your foot
against a stone.
Psalm 91: 10-12*

"See that you do not despise
one of these little ones;
for I tell you,
the angels in heaven
always behold the face
of my Father in heaven."
Matthew 18:10

Chapter 2

A Soul Connection

The soul is the principle of life, feeling, thought and action in humans. It is regarded as a distinct entity separate from the body and commonly held to be separable in existence from the body; it is the spiritual part of humans as distinct from the physical part. Basically, your being is like a car, and your mind is like the engine of the car and your soul is the petrol. Our soul body connects with angels. You do not have to invite angels into your life because they are already with you. But for the most part, people are not connecting with them.

A soul, being invisible by nature, can be distinguished only by the presence of its body or bodies. The mere presence of a body signifies that its existence is made possible by unfulfilled desires. So long as the soul of the man is encased in one, two or three body containers, sealed tightly with the corks of ignorance and desires, he cannot merge with the sea of spirit.

Look at our children. Look at what is happening to their bodies, souls and minds. This is the war on the streets of our cities. When you see children on drugs, depressed or suicidal it is as if they are wasting away and there is no light in their eyes. This is the real battle for souls. When you destroy the body, the chemistry, the spiritual centres, you destroy the ability to connect to higher vibrations. That is what drugs do; they are the death of the soul.

We have traced man's ascent from the appearance of the embryonic soul to the state of the spiritually advanced through the stages of evolving consciousness from the life of sensation to the life of thought. We have seen him retread the cycle of birth and death in the three worlds, each world yielding him its harvest and offering him progress. We are now in a position to follow him into the final stages of his human evolution, stages that lie in the future for the vast bulk of our humanity, but that have already been trodden by its eldest children, and that are being by its eldest children and that are being trodden by a slender number of men and women in our own day.

As the mind obeys the soul, so must the lower nature obey the mind. The astral body forms the bridge over the gulf which separates consciousness from the physical brain. In the astral body it is karma, feeling, enjoying, suffering. We shall find it in yet other aspects, as we pass to higher plans, but the fundamental idea is the same throughout and serves us as guiding clues in this most tangled world.

Just as souls may be delayed in their progress by foolish and inconsiderate friends, so may they be aided in it by wise and well directed efforts. Hence all religions enjoy the use of 'prayers for the dead'. These prayers with their accompanying ceremonies are more or less useful according to the knowledge, the love and the will power by which they are ensouled.

The physical, astral and mental planes are 'the three worlds through which lies the pilgrimage of the soul, again and again repeated. In these three worlds revolves the wheel of human life and souls are bound to that wheel through their evolution and are carried by it to each of these worlds in turn. To the realms that lie beyond we now may turn.

"A tree is like a saint. It calls no one to itself, nor does it send anyone away. It offers to protect everyone who wants to come to it, whether this be a man, a woman, a child, or an animal".

Anandamayi Ma

I believe that each of us possesses a soul that exists after the death of the physical body. And that this soul returns time and time again to other bodies, in a progressive effort to reach a higher plane. I also believe this is not the only place where there are souls. There are many dimensions, many different levels of consciousness where there are souls. There is no limit to energy. The soul does not have DNA.

Buddhists and Hindus have been accumulating past life cases for thousands of years. Reincarnation was written off in the New Testament until the time of Constantine, where the Romans censored it. Jesus himself may have believed in it, for he asked the Apostles if they recognised John the Baptist as Elijah returned; Elijah had lived nine hundred years before John. It is a tenet of Jewish mysticism; in some sects it was standard teaching until the early nineteenth century. I no longer doubt that reincarnation is real. Our souls have lived before and will live again. That is our immortality.

The soul exists outside of time. The perspective of the soul is immense, and the perception of the soul is without limitations of the personality. Souls that have chosen the physical experience of life as we know it – as a path of evolution – have, in general, incarnated their energies many times into many psychological and physical forms. For each incarnation, the soul creates a different personality. Each personality contributes, in its own special way with its own special aptitudes and lessons to learn – consciously or unconsciously – to the evolution of its soul.

The personality and its body are artificial aspects of the soul. When they have served their functions, at the end of the soul's incarnation, the soul releases them. They come to an end, but the soul does not. After an incarnation, the soul returns to its immortal and timeless state. It returns once again to its natural state of compassion, clarity and boundless love. The continual incarnation and reincarnation of the energy of the soul into physical reality for the purposes of healing or balancing its energy, is in accordance with the Law of Karma.

The framework of Karma and reincarnation is impersonal, and provides for each soul – in response to the actions of its personalities – the experiences that it requires in order to evolve.

Just before we die, our soul – that part of us that is aware when it leaves the body – pauses for a moment, floating. In that state it can differentiate colour, hear voices, identify objects, and review the life it has just departed. This phenomenon is called an out-of-body experience. It has been documented thousands of times. Each of us experiences it when we die, but only a few have come back to present life to report on it.

The soul is timeless. Ultimately there is probably just one soul, one energy. Many people call this God.

I see the soul as a body of energy that blends with universal energy, then splits off again, intact when it returns to a new life, before it merges with the One. It looks down on the body it has left and conducts what I call a life review, meaning a review of the life just departed. Your soul registers its experience. Once the soul has finished its review, it seems to go further from your body, often finding the light. This may not happen immediately. The light is always there and sometimes there are other souls around – they are masters or guides and they can help your soul on its journey towards the One. At some level, your soul merges with the light. Our souls are all the same age, which is ageless, but some souls advance more quickly than others. We are immoral. We are eternal. Our souls will never die.

"When you make two one, and when you make the inside like the outside and the outside like the inside, and the above like the below, then you will enter the Kingdom".

The Gospel of Thomas.

It is not your imagination, angels are among us, now more than ever. God sends angels to help us heal ourselves, our lives and our world. The angels are powerful healers and you can work with them to help speed up their healing efforts. The more we invite angels into our lives, the more readily our lives reflect the splendour of heaven. There are no limits to their power. Angels can help us heal our relationships, cancer, careers, finances, housing issues, and any other challenges in our life. We simply need to connect with them.

"Feel God in the temple of each thought that is born within your mind, in every feeling born within your heart, every aspiration born within your soul".

– Swami Yogananda

Some people build altars in their home with statues of their favourite saints, holy pictures and place a vase of fresh flowers there daily. Sometimes they add photos of their ancestors, a selection of crystals, decks of angel cards. They clear and declutter, and make room for uplifting light and energy to flow through their home. This is a beautiful way to allow the angel's presence into your life.

To really connect with your angels, they require you to surrender to God, to be pure in body and mind. Simply have faith in God and be open minded to the possibility that there is an angel standing right beside you, waiting to help you on your journey. Consider lighting a candle on your altar.

When I light a candle, angels instantly come to me.

When you have lit the candle, sit and relax. Close your eyes and invite angels into your presence. Remember you must be focused, humble and kind.

> *"Your time is limited, so don't waste it living someone else's life. Don't be trapped by dogma — which is living with the results of other people's thinking. Don't let the noise of others' opinions drown out your own inner voice. And most important, have the courage to follow your heart and intuition."*
>
> *– Steve Jobs*

You need to treat your angels just like your ancestors. They need love, respect and discipline. You need to show them care. Their love for you is powerful and unconditional. You can ask God to send angels to you, or call upon the angels directly. The angels always answer to God's will. Trust simply in God.

God's will is that you be happy. When you are enjoying a cup of tea, make a cup for them. Many of my own angels love English Breakfast tea, and some of my angels love a cup of black coffee. Place it on the altar. I always keep a glass of water on my altar for them to take a sip when they are thirsty. I like to spoil my angels by giving them sweets and a slice of Victoria sponge cake. Sometimes, while I enjoy a cup of tea myself (and make a cup for them) I simply sit and talk to my angels. I have found that the more I connect with my angels, the more blessings I receive in my life.

I am fortunate to see my angels. Usually however, you cannot see your angels. Only people who have made a connection with their angels can see them. If you wish to see your angles, first try to connect with invisible souls. For example, you might visit St. Patrick's Cathedral, then come home and pray to him and light a candle on your altar to him. The saint will then guide the angels to you. Saints are very close to God, and angels are close to saints. When you connect with a saint, he or she will send you an army of angels to help you. Whenever you are in difficulty, say "Jesus help me," and he will send you angels to help you. Wherever they see injustice, they will help.

Angels want to guide us in the right direction. They are like our spiritual GPS system. They guide us through our inner voice. When you begin to connect with your angels, simply ask them for help. Angels are brilliant listeners. They listen and never judge. You can speak to angels out loud or internally in your mind. Rest assured that either way, they will be listening. By simply asking your angels for help, you allow them to help you.

No person is truly alone, those we have loved echo still within our thoughts, our words, our hearts, our spirit and our dreams"
Anonymous

You deserve to receive God's love and support from the angels as much as anyone. When you push away the help the angels offer you, it is often because you are afraid that you do not deserve it. Loving yourself can feel hard, but in fact it is easy. It does not even require your permission because of our soul-to-soul connection. When you forget to ask the angels for help or for the answers to your prayers, their mission is delayed. The angels support you as part of God's plan.

Angels prefer to move at night time when it is dark as they do not like the light, but they can come anytime to guide you. As God has appointed angels to live in the astral plane. They can visit you in seconds as they are running on high-speed cosmic fuel. The way humans live in the human world, angels live in the spirit world.

There is probably nothing more tragic than saying goodbye to a child. Yet children's souls are in heaven. Children five years old or younger have no concept of death the way we do.

When infants and children pass over, they do not realise that they are dead. Since they do not know that they have passed on, they rush to the aid of their bereaved family, offering them etheric gifts.

Children who are aborted do not blame their parents, and they do not realise that they are dead either. In fact, the souls of those children who do not grow to full term births because of abortion or miscarriage, or stillbirth stay by their mothers' sides. Their souls have "first dibs" on the next body that the mother conceives, so, if you have lost an infant or foetus and have since had another child, the chances are that this is the same soul. If the woman does not conceive additional children, that soul then grows up next to the mother and acts as a spirit guide. The child's spirit may enter the physical world and come into its mother's family in another way, such as through adoption, or by becoming her niece or nephew.

Prayer For Healing After an Abortion

Loving Lord, I come to You and confess my sin of abortion, and ask that Your healing grace would touch my heart today. The remembrance of it is eating me inside and I need Your healing grace and loving forgiveness.

I cast this great burden onto You, knowing that You have promised to heal those that are broken-hearted and to bind up the inner of those that are hurting.

I know that the consequences of our wrong choices can bring much pain, but I also know that You are a God Who promised to forgive and heal all who come to You with a contrite heart and that You will remember our sins no more.

Forgive me Lord, heal my life. Create in me a clean heart I pray, and renew a right spirit within me. This I ask in Jesus' name, Amen.

Prayer for Babies in the Womb

Heavenly Father, I bring before You all women that are pregnant, and all couples that are expecting a little baby to be born into their home. I ask for your protection for all babies that are secretly being formed in the womb of their mother.

I ask for their protection, preservation and healthy growth while still developing in the womb, and I pray that expectant mothers will be given the wisdom and grace to avoid the things that can prove so detrimental to the development of the pre-born child.

I pray that You would surround all pre-born babies with a hedge of protection, and that each little life may develop into a perfectly healthy new-born baby, knowing that there are so many problems that can affect a child in the womb and injure their physical and cognitive development.

Lord it was You that said, "suffer the little children to come unto Me and forbid them not", and so I pray that each one would be born into a family that loves and cherishes them and that each one would learn of Jesus in the days that lie ahead. In Jesus' name, Amen

"As thou knowest not what is the way of the spirit, nor how the bone do grow in the womb of her that is with child: even so thou knowest not the works of God who maketh all."

(Ecclesiastes 11:5)

Prayer for Healing my Heart after a miscarriage

Dear Lord, I am overwhelmed with sadness because I have lost the baby that was growing in my womb. I was so excited about bringing her/him into the world. Now I will not be able to enjoy and share those beautiful moments with this child. Even though I don't understand, I trust in your word, which says that all things work together for good. So I know that all things are working out together for good. In Jesus' name, I believe and pray, Amen.

As difficult as it might be to accept, your child may have made the decision to go home to heaven before you were ready for him or her to leave. Be comforted that children are never alone in heaven. Grandparents, aunts, uncles, pets and other children surround any child who has passed away.

Usually, children live on the other side with relatives whom they knew on earth. When a child dies from suicide, it is frowned upon in heaven, because it is wasting a body that could be used in service of the light. However, no one judges suicide victims. Angels and guides surround these individuals with doctor and mental health counsellor angels. Praying for their soul also gives them healing.

And still her grief would not abate.
at last she bore another child, and great
Was the father's joy; and his cry: "A Son!".
That day, to this rejoice – he was the only one.
Dejected and wanted the mother to lay; her soul was numb...
Then suddenly she cried with anguish wild,
Her thoughts less on the new than on the absent child...
"My angel is in his grave, and I'm not at his side!"
Speaking through the babe now held in her embrace
She hears again the well-known voice adored:
"Tis I, - but do not tell!" He gazes at her face
-Victor Hugo

The angels protect you like a mother protects her baby in the womb. Angels never die. They complete their time, reincarnate and go to God's kingdom.

The world is ruled by angels and devils. When an angel sees you living in a nice clean home with a good environment, when they see you praying and doing good deeds for friends, they want to connect with you.

These angels give you thousands of messages – it is up to you to work with your angels and decode the messages they send. They can do this by putting a song on your car radio, or flashing a light on and off.

Finding white feathers is an especially powerful sign. A warm sensation or a flashing light is a clear sign of angels. A tingling sensation on your skin is a further validation of the presence of angels. Look up to the sky and see angel clouds; these may look like an angel, or like another symbol that has meaning and significance for you. Scent is a commonly used sign from your ancestors or loved ones who have crossed over. Finding coins on your path is another sign.

When you learn to understand the signs, you will begin to pay close attention to the messages the angels are sending you. It's only then that you can understand and work with your angels in both the business and spiritual balance in your life. Angels are sent by God to help you, love you, support you and guide you in all these things.

There are seven main archangels, arguably the closest beings to God. Archangels are incredibly powerful beings of the spiritual realm. They watch over humanity and other angels, but also over various aspects of the universe itself.

First among them is Archangel Michael, whose name translates as 'he who is like God.' He is viewed as being the lead archangel. His main role in our world is to promote courage, bravery and justice. He also protects us to keep evil spirits from leading us away from our spiritual path.

I have a deep connection with Archangel Michael, firstly because I was called after him. His feast day is 29th September and my birthday is the 28th September. It was the power of visiting Archangel Michael's well in Ballinskelligs that set me on the discovery of Kingdom Water. After being chosen by Archangel Michael for this journey, he introduced me to Michael from Southern Scientific, who tested the water found on my family land for me.

Prayer to Archangel Michael

Saint-Michael Archangel,
Defend us in the day of battle;
Be our safeguard
against the wickedness
And snares of the devil.
May God rebuke him,
We humbly pray And do thou
O prince of the Heavenly Host,
By the power of God,
Cast into hell Satan.
And all the other evil spirits
Who prowl through the world
Seeking the ruin of souls.

In my previous book, The Discovery of Kingdom Water, I wrote about a trip to Lourdes, when I called in to an old shop where the shopkeeper had a fabulous collection of prayers to Archangel Michael. The shopkeeper was reading a book on Saint Michael. I told her all about the water found on my land and my journey, and she said that Archangel Michael was making all of this happen. She gave me a copy of the book she was reading. Among the angelic visions I regularly receive about the water, the signs from Archangel Michael are the most powerful.

Archangel Michael is deeply connected to the sun and carries the energy of electrical fire, so any time you are connecting with Archangel Michael, there is a likelihood of seeing flashes of light, sparkles of light on water, or blueish purple orbs. All these are signs of Archangel Michael. The spiritual connection with Archangel Michael is very strong in Kerry, particularly in Ballinskelligs, part of the Dingle Diamond. Skellig Michael, a very sacred place, is at a conjunction between two important ley lines, both of which connect with sites of great spirituality – many named after Saint Michael, including St. Michael's mount, Mont St. Michel and St. Michael's Well.

Angels are the messengers of God. They are gifts to us from God and communicate to us from Him. They work in conjunction with your higher self and your soul's alignment. The angels don't judge your beliefs or play mind games. Instead, they work with your thoughts as a way to reach you. The angels, along with our higher self, will never defy God's will.

I always trust my gut feeling. This has never let me down. I have reached that state of trust with the angels in their emotional and physical feelings. God and the angels speak to us in response to our queries – we can direct a question to them and they will respond within a day or so. Sometimes you hear the answer in a song, or read it in a newspaper or see it as part of a TV advert. Keep repeating the question until you get an answer.

On this journey with Kingdom Water, the angels first showed themselves to me as orbs of light. Then they began showing me telepathic messages in the shapes of rocks, and pictures of my grandmother's face. They guided me on how to open the seven hidden water springs against all the odds. Seeing angel lights is a very real and normal experience, but many people are reluctant to publicly admit this fact as they fear they will not be believed.

Angel clouds are also very common. If you notice such a thing, it is another way of God letting you know that the angels are with you. This happens to me often. Sometimes they let me take photos, other times it is for my eyes only.

The angels send signs to people to let them know they are nearby – random coins and feathers or a light flickering in your home, these are signs that your angels are nearby and are saying hello. When a loved one passes, they will often send a sign in the shape of a bird such as a robin, or butterflies, or certain specific flowers that you would recognise. Anyone can receive messages from their angels. Allow yourself to be open. They will not tell you anything you cannot handle. They will not try to control your life either. Their messages help you to feel secure and happier in every aspect of your life. You can ask the angels to help you in anything, from finding a new home to help with parenting. When you learn to start working with your angels, you will function better in your life, and it will become simpler and more peaceful.

Prayers of the Angel

My God, I believe, I adore, I hope and I love You!
I ask pardon of You for those
Who do not believe, do not adore, do not hope and do not love You!
Most Holy Trinity, Father, Son and Holy Spirit,
I adore You profoundly, and I offer you
the most precious Body, Blood, Soul and Divinity of Jesus Christ, present
in all the tabernacles of the world,
in reparation for the outrages, sacrileges and indifference
with which He Himself is offended.
And, through the infinite merits of His most Sacred Heart,
And the Immaculate Heart of Mary,
I beg of You the conversion of poor sinners.
Amen.

I have been chosen by the angels to bring the ancient wells on my family land to the light of day, I give gratitude to them. I vibrate pure positive energy throughout the universe. The angels are naturally attracted to positive energy, reaching out to these frequencies from people on earth. Giving thanks to your angels will help build a two-way relationship with the hard-working angel that cares for you.

When I meditate and pray, I simply say thanks to the angels for giving me this water and bringing this blessing into my life. Every time I see a rainbow, or a rainbow orb around the moon, or a double rainbow appears where it has not been raining, I know these are signs from my angels, bringing encouragement from the heavens. Recently the angels showed me the number 7 everywhere I looked. This was a powerful sign of their guidance and wisdom. The number 7 is very powerful, and the angels have sent me this as congratulations that I am finally in tune with my true self and on the right path in my journey through the universe.

So invite angels into your life. Talk to them and listen to them, and when they respond be grateful and thank them. Be open to their presence and help, and you too can find an angel on your shoulder. You may even find that your life is transformed, like mine has been on this exciting journey in the discovery of Kingdom Water.

Prayers for Guidance

May God, the Lord, bless us and make us perfect and holy in his sight.
May the riches of his glory abound in us.
May he instruct us with the word of truth,
inform us with the gospel of salvation,
and enrich us with his love;
thorough Christ our Lord.
Amen

Chapter 3

Ganges River of Angels

Winding 1,560 miles across Northern India, from the Himalaya mountains to the Indian Ocean, the Ganges River is not a sacred place; it is a sacred entity. Known as Ganga Na – Mother Ganges – the river is revered as a goddess whose purity cleans the sins of the faithful and aids the dead on their path to heaven. The Ganges is a sacred river of the Hindus. When the Hindus die, they all want their ashes scattered in this sacred river. The sacred rites of the Asthi Visarjan Ceremony can be performed.

Cremation is an important part of our view of destiny, embracing a symbolic form of the human embryo, which Hindus believe began with the male seed developing into bones and the female blood resulting in flesh. At the end of one's life a reversal takes place as the heat of the funeral pyre divides flesh from bones. The flames of the cremation fire are the means by which the human form, or body, is presented to God as a last sacrifice. The spirit is released from the body for its journey, shaped by the individual's good (or Karma) during his or her life. So, while ashes go to the Ganges the soul does not have to go back to the body. The Hindus believe that if a deceased's ashes are laid in the Ganges at Varanasi, their soul will be transported back to heaven, and will escape the cycle of rebirth. In a culture that believes in reincarnation, this concept, called Moksha, is profound. The holier the place the better the chances your soul will achieve Moksha and avoid returning to earth as a cow or a cricket in the next life.

There are many, many stories about the Ganges. One involves King Sagara. In Hindu mythology, King Sagara was a prominent King of the Suryavansha dynasty in Vidarbha, the north-eastern region of the Indian state of Maharashtra.

According to the Bhagavata Purana, when King Bahuka lost his kingdom due to the treachery of his relatives, he, along with his wives, retired to the forest. Soon the king died, leaving behind his wives, one of whom was pregnant. When the pregnant wife was going to burn herself with the dead, King Sage Aurva prevented her from doing so.

When the co-wives got news of her pregnancy, they fed her poison, but the child was born with the poison, hence the name Sagara (Sa – meaning with, Gara – meaning poison).

One day King Sagara asked his guru what he had done to receive the comfortable life of a king. His guru replied that in his previous birth Sagara was a poor Brahmin, but he had a daughter and he arranged a marriage for his daughter, hence performing Kanyadan (donation or gift of a maiden), which is considered to be one of the highest virtues of life.

Hearing this Sagara was surprised that he had only given his daughter's hand in marriage and in return was able to enjoy a royal comfort life. He decided to do tapu (austerities) to beget 60,000 daughters. But Lord Indra (King of Devas), the leader of the demigods, feared that performing the marriage of 60,000 daughters would make Sagara attain Indra's throne, so he requested Goddess Saraswati, Goddess of Wisdom, to sit on Sagara's tongue and when he asked for the boon, to change the

"Putri" (daughter) word into "Putra" (Son). Sarawati accepted and did this, and so Sagara received 60,000 sons instead of daughters.

Years later, King Sagara performed a horse sacrifice ritual to prove his supremacy. Lord Indra became fearful over the results of the ritual, so he decided to steal the horse. He left the horse at the ashram of Kapila, who was in deep meditation. King Sagar's 60,000 sons (born of Queen Sumati), and his son Asamanja (born of Queen Keshini) were then sent to find the horse. When the 60,000 sons found the horse at Kapiladeva's ashram, they thought Kapila, the meditating rishi (sage), had stolen it. When they prepared to attack, Kapila opened his eyes. Because the sons of King Sagara had disrespected such a great personality, fire emanated from their own bodies, and those 60,000 sons were immediately burned to ashes.

Generations later, one of Sagara's descendant, Bhagiratha felt sad about his forefathers death and he performed tapa to Goddess Ganga to come from the heavens to the earth so that his forefathers could be freed from the world.

Hinduism is the world's oldest religion and to quote from the Mahabharata:

'Verily, Ganga is the path to heaven of those who have bathed in her current.'

On my journey of discovering Kingdom Water I had the pleasure of visiting the Ganges. Walking across the suspension bridge over the Ganges was something special. I stood still for a moment to take in my surroundings. Around me, little riverbank shops were selling everything from plastic souvenirs to Smeg fridges.

I reached the river itself and followed the instructions given to me by my Guruji: 'just sit and pray and be sure to bathe in the water and pray to holy Ganga with the following prayer:

Holy Mother, please, Mother, I am so grateful to you for giving me the chance to visit you. I myself and my near and dear, and my ancestors, those not in physical form, on behalf of them I am praying to you. Please accept my prayer."

I was told to be very careful near the riverside as the current is fast, and there are many angels present.

I said the prayer that my Guruji had told me. I had brought a small bottle of Kingdom Water with me, and I poured it into the Ganges and got the blessings of the Ganges. This brought a wonderfully liberating and spiritual feeling. It was so powerful to know that Kingdom Water was now flowing through the Ganges. I sat down on a step and prayed.

As I did so, a voice inside my head said, "Look at the water." When I did, I saw many angels.

Then, as it began to get dark, in the distance a light flickered on and off. A voice in my head said 'keep watching.' With that, an angel some 20ft high appeared, flapping her wings. I went to take a photo, but the photo came out blank. Then Our Lady appeared to me, with Saint Martin, Saint Padre Pio, Neem Baba Karoli, along with my Guruji and Steve Jobs. I could not believe what I was seeing. Then I saw a man wearing a Stetson hat who I had seen before in visions. The faces of those who had appeared flashed three times. I saw my grandmother, Mary Bridget, and finally Our Lord, on a crucifix. It was utterly overwhelming and emotional; a million different emotions wrapped into one.

Along came a young boy then, and gave me a bowl of food to feed the fish, which I did. I was given a blessing from one of the priests known as 'Pandas'.

Because of the purifying nature of the river, Hindus believe that any rituals performed at the banks of the Ganges will bring fortune and wash away impurity. There are seven sacred rivers in India, of which the holiest is the Ganges. The water of the Ganges originates in the frozen heart of the Himalayas. The river travels thousands of miles across the plains before flowing east into Bangladesh and from there spilling into the Bay of Bengal. Mother Ganga is described by ancient Hindu scriptures as a gift from the Gods – the earthly incarnation of the deity Ganga. It is, above all, the river of India, and has held India's heart captive and drawn uncounted millions to her banks since the dawn of history.

For thousands of years the Ganges has been held sacred and is repeatedly invoked in sacred Hindu texts including Vedas, Mahabharat and Ramayana. The river Ganga is not just a river, it is an all-giving and all-forgiving Mother. The Hindus call it 'Ganga Maiyya' with love and devotion. The river takes on the form of a sacred goddess who absolves all the sins gathered in a lifetime. Mother Ganga takes everyone into her loving embrace after death.

So holy is the water of the Ganges that people travel to her shores to bless the remains of their loved ones in it. Her waters are considered so pure and so powerful that a person is washed of all sins and becomes eligible for entry to heaven by the simple act of pouring a handful of water from the river over one's head and letting it run down over the body.

Moving, flowing or falling water is believed to have great cleansing powers. Water absorbs pollution, but when it is flowing, like a river, it carries pollution away. The word Ganga is derived from 'Gan' meaning 'to go' and indeed, Ganga is the swift-goer and the energetic movement of the water is constantly mentioned as one reason for her purifying attributes. Ganga's fall from heaven is replicated daily in thousands of Hindu temples where water from the Ganges river is poured over the sacred Shiva Linga.

Ganga water is used in all Hindu prayers and ceremonies. Before someone dies, Ganga water is placed in their mouths. Just as in Ireland holy water is used to bless people and homes, in India Ganga water is used to purify a house and those who are in it.

Hindus view the Ganges as a birthplace of the divine. The river is believed to be a crack in the physical world where the supernatural can slip through to immerse us mortals in its wonders. Ganga water is also used for medicinal purposes as it contains many minerals and passes through many plants and herbs. Most people who come to the Ganges do so because they have a spiritual thirst they want to quench. Quite simply, the river Ganges is the river of heaven.

I decided to bathe in the water, observing the Ganga Aarti devotional ritual as I did so. This involves a small *diya* with a candle and flowers that is floated down the river. The offering is made to the Goddess Ganga. This is utterly unique. Being at the side of the Holy River is a once in a lifetime experience.

As I bathed, I marvelled at the fact that the water was much cleaner than I had expected. Bathing there was a raw, intense feeling. Such an experience will leave a mark on your soul and change how you think about life. It will stay with me forever. As I grasped the rope that is placed to help bathers out of the water, the figure 7 appeared on the pillar next to my left hand, and I was able to take a photo of it. I was also lucky enough to get a few beautiful photos of some angels that appeared to me in the sky.

I filled two bottles of water to bring home to bless my seven springs with. As I left the Ganges, I noticed a gorgeous hotel called the Ramkund Resort that has the best location and the best views – the perfect place for anyone wanting to stay and wake up to breath-taking views over the river.

I spent nearly three hours there. We were heading back to Delhi that night by car, and I left the Ganges with a heavy heart. It was night-time and the roads were quiet. We passed through much rough terrain. We passed towns including Rishikesh, home to the most difficult and exhilarating white water rafting. It's in the foothills of the Himalayas, and I decided that on any future visit, this would certainly be on my bucket list.

It began to rain as we drove and for a moment, looking out the window, I felt I was back home and not 8,500 miles from Knocknagoshel. I could not help but think of the great Babaji who would typically start his day around 3am, with a bath, often in the cold River Ganges, which was followed by meditation or a fire ceremony. Around 5am he would see his devotees for ceremonial Chandan (placing a mark on forehead), followed by morning Aarti (devotional singing) around 6am. Then, until noon, everybody would be engaged in some form of karma yoga. At noon, the only meal of the day was being served, followed by more karma yoga in the afternoon. Sometimes a more elaborate ceremony such as the fire ritual haven would be performed around the noon time. In the afternoon, Babaji would sometimes see the devotees for individual audiences, known as darshan. Then there would be another bath, followed by the evening Aarti. After the evening Aarti, Babaji was giving short speeches that were recorded in "The Teachings of Babaji".

"In this, Ganga water is not required.
No special utensils are necessary.
Even flowers are redundant.
In this puja all gods have disappeared.
And emptiness has emerged with euphoria"

Lahiri Mahasaya

O Adorable Mother Ganges!
by Sri Swami Sivananda

O adorable Mother Ganga, the Shakti of Lord Siva, Prostrations and adorations unto Thee!
Thou art the creatrix and nourisher of the world. People address Thee as "Bhagirathi", "Har Gange",

I know well Thy story, O dear Mother,
Once King Bhagiratha brought Thee down
To purify the ashes of his grandfathers,
Lord Siva took Thee in His matted locks,
Thou takest origin in Gaumukh, beyond Gangotri,
Thou passest through Uttarkashi, Rishikesh and Haridwar,
Thou purifiest the Punyabhumi of Bharata Varsha;
Thou finally mergest in Ganga Sagar;

Thou art Bhrantinashini and Jagatjanani;

Thou adornest the head of Gangadhar,
Thou art the nectar of immortality that gives salvation,
Thou art Mahamaya, Adishakti and Avyaktam,
People sing "Gange Lahari" in the evening,
They do Arati with Bhav and devotion;
They raise Jaya Jayakar: "Ganga Mai Ki Jai!",
They worship Thee with flowers and Prasad,
Thou art Jnana Ganga, the wisdom nectar,
Thy subtle form is in the celestial regions,
Thy gross form only human beings behold here,
Thou persuadest the world as subtle Chidakasa,
Thou hast attracted the people of the whole world,
Thy name has holy associations and vibrations,
A dip in Thee refreshes and purifies the heart,
Millions flock to Thee during Kumbh Mela,
Thou art the purest water on earth,
No germs can thrive in Thee,
This is the finding of the scientist in his laboratory,
Thou art sparkling and clear as crystal,
A drop on the tongue at the moment of death gives Moksha,

Yogis and Sadhus do Tapas on Thy banks in cottages,
Thou deliverest them from the rounds of births and deaths,
Who can describe, O Mother, Thy glory and splendour?
Will a day come to me, Beloved Mother,
To sit on a block of stone on Thy bank,
To shed continuous tears of Prem on Thy lap,
And merge in Thee for ever and ever?
O all-powerful Mother of compassion and love,
Bless me with Thy Grace and mercy,
Destroy my darkness and ignorance,
Remove the veil and show Thy true form,
I am thine, O Mother, Thou art mine,
The sense of duality has vanished now,
The bridge that separates us has broken now,
Let me dwell in Thee, Mother, for ever and ever

Many famous Hollywood celebrities have visited the Ganges. Julia Roberts fell in love with India and Hinduism when she filmed 'Eat Pray Love.' She visited the Ganges and asked Elizabeth Gilbert, author of the book Eat Pray Love, "Is this when you forgave yourself?"

From attending the morning Aarti on the ghats of Vrindavan and Varanasi to strolling on the streets of Majhura, Hollywood stars have come to the Ganges for peace and enlightenment. Whether they come to India for a film shoot or a 'life conference', the one common thread connecting their visits has been that they have always been spiritual journeys.

Hollywood superstar Sylvester Stallone visited Haridwar to perform the Tithi Ashirvaadh virtual for his son Sage who died in 2012 of a heart attack.

The Beatles – John Lennon, Paul McCartney, George Harrison and Ringo Starr – visited the Ganges in 1968 while studying transcendental meditation. While in Rishikesh they composed a song called 'The Happy Rishikesh Song'.

On November 9th 2013 Prince Charles and Camilla Parker Bowles visited Parmarth Niketan, Rishikesh to take part in the Ganga Aarti.

"I wish I could have never left Rishikesh, I fell in love with the Aura of the City".

Prince Charles

In 2006 Hollywood Superstar Brad Pitt travelled to Varanasi to watch the morning Aarti and experience a boat ride in the Ganga. Pitt was left 'awestruck'. "*I found Varanasi absolutely staggering. I have never seen anything like it before. The City just spills into the River Ganges. It's a holy place where people go to die. It's really, really extraordinary!*".

Brad Pitt

In 2012 Ashton Kutcher backpacked across Mathura while shooting the biopic movie of Apple co-founder Steve Jobs. Kutcher spent a few days on the ghats of Vrindavan shooting screens from Jobs' life when he came to India to attain enlightenment.

Hollywood stars Richard Gere, Pierce Brosnan, Sharon Stone and Demi Moore travelled in January 2001 to India for the holy ceremony of cleansing in the Ganges River.

Chapter 4

Archangels

The Archangels oversee the guardian angels. They are usually larger, stronger and more powerful. There are seven archangels recognised in the Judeo-Christian tradition. Medieval cosmology included seven archangels to correspond to the seven planets that were known at the time, and the seven days of the week. The lists of archangels and their corresponding planets and days are as diverse as any other catalogue of things angelic.

There are nine archangels that are cited in the Kabbalah. New age angel-ologists associate a different archangel with each of the twelve signs of the Zodiac.

Archangel Michael
Archangel Michael's name means "Who is like God", which signifies his rank as the greatest of angels. Michael teaches us to be spiritual warriors, to fiercely guard our integrity and ruthlessly cut out any attachments or beliefs that do not serve our ultimate good. Even in heaven St. Michael is mighty among the angels. The Book of Revelation (12:7-17) depicts him as the commander of the heavenly host of angels as they battle Satan

and the rebellious spirits. The church celebrates the feast of St. Michael and all angels on September 29th. St. Michael is patron saint of grocers, mariners, paratroopers, police officers and military personnel.

Prayer to St. Michael

Saint Michael, the Archangel, defend us in battle.
Be our protection against the wickedness and snares of the devil.
May God rebuke him, we humbly pray, and do thou,
O Prince of the heavenly host, by the power of God,
cast into hell Satan and all evil spirits who prowl
about the world seeking the ruin of souls.
Amen.

Visions of Archangel Michael have been reported by many saints, but the most famous were those experienced by Joan of Arc. In the Fifteenth Century, Archangel Michael appeared to Joan and told her she had been chosen to help the King of France reclaim his Kingdom. At a decisive point in the Hundred Years War between England and France, when all seemed lost, Archangel Michael gave Joan of Arc strength, courage and determination to go forward. By the power of faith that Archangel Michael imparted to Joan, the forces roared in defence of the flame of liberty. Joan of Arc later testified before the clerics about Archangel Michael and his angels, '*I have seen them with my corporeal eyes, as plainly as I see you*'.

A number of historical and scriptural accounts give evidence that people of various spiritual traditions have counted on Archangel Michael for protection. In earlier times, people had a much greater awareness of angels than we have today.

In the Dead Sea Scroll, the war of the sons of light against the sons of darkness, Archangel Michael is called Prince of Light through whom God promises to 'send perpetual help to the sons of light'. Archangel

Michael is known in Islamic traditions as Mikail, the Angel of Nature who provides both food and knowledge to man.

According to Jewish mystical tradition, Archangel Michael was the angel who wrestled with Jacob. He guided Israel through the wilderness, brought the plagues upon the Pharaoh, parted the red sea, destroyed the armies of Sennacherib in the fiery furnace. He appeared to Joshua as he prepared to lead the Israelites in battle at Jericho. The Book of Enoch notes that Archangel Michael commanded the nations. Everywhere we go we find Archangel Michael. 'Make yourself familiar with the Angels, and behold them frequently in spirit; for without being seen, they are present with you'. *Saint Frances de Sales*

Archangel Michael

O Mighty Prince of the Heavenly Hosts, St. Michael,
we beg you to protect and defend us in struggles against the everyday
temptations in this world. Help us to overcome all evils and strengthen us,
that we may declare our faith in and loyalty to the Most High
so that together with all the angels and saints in heaven
we may glorify the Lord. St. Michael, please intercede for us together with
the Blessed Virgin Mary, and obtain for us the following requests
(Here Mention Requests)

Present to God the Father all these petitions through Jesus Christ our Lord
together with the Holy Spirit forever and ever. Amen.

One of the ways we can commune with our Archangels is by going into their spiritual home, or retreat. All of the Archangels as well as other beings of the light that minister to the earth have retreats. They are located in the realm of light as well as this dense world – in the realm known as the etheric octave or heaven world.

Your soul can retreat when your body sleeps. You simply ask Archangel Michael and their legions of angels to take you to their retreat and to protect your soul as you travel there. While you are in the retreat you can receive and experience an invigorating spiritual recharge. When this happens, often we wake up and think it was a dream, but many times it was probably not a dream at all. It was a real experience where we met beings of light, teachers, avatars, angels, ascended masters and though we may not have a specific memory of it, something has happened on a profound level of our being. Portions of the experience may show up in our outer awareness as insights, new creativity or a deeper understanding on connecting with Archangels and Angels.

This world is a battlefield and within ourselves there is often a battle. We can see the consequences in the lives of those who make wrong choices. We pray to our angels for protection for ourselves. All heavenly beings have an electronic presence which is their auric field and emanation. It is composed of force fields of light that comprise the individual identity. That presence can be duplicated without limit. So heavenly beings can appear to anyone upon earth or to a million people simultaneously.

The Chaplet Novena of Saint Michael

Incline unto my aid, O God.
O Lord, make haste to help me.
Glory be to the Father…

Then recite, beginning on the first separate bead:

1. By the intercession of St. Michael and the heavenly choir of the Seraphims, may it please God to make us worthy to receive into our hearts the fire of His perfect charity. Amen.

Our Father, Three Hail Marys

1. By the intercession of St. Michael and the heavenly choir of the Cherubims, may God in His mercy grant us grace to abandon the ways of sin, and follow the path of Christian perfection. Amen.

Our Father, Three Hail Marys

1. By the intercession of St. Michael and the sacred choir of the Thrones, may it please God to infuse into our hearts the spirit of true and sincere humility. Amen.

Our Father, Three Hail Marys

1. By the intercession of St. Michael and the heavenly choir of the Dominions, may it please God to grant us grace to have dominion over our senses, and to correct our immoral passions. Amen.

Our Father, three Hail Marys

1. By the intercession of St. Michael and the heavenly choir of the Powers, may God grant that we keep our souls from the wiles and temptations of the devil. Amen.

Our Father, three Hail Marys

1. By the intercession of St. Michael and the admirable heavenly Virtues, may it please God to keep us from falling into temptation, and may he deliver us from evil. Amen.

Our Father, Three Hail Marys

1. By the intercession of St. Michael and the heavenly choir of Principalities, may it please God to fill our souls with the spirit of true and sincere obedience. Amen.

Our Father, Three Hail Marys

1. By the intercession of St. Michael and the heavenly choir of the Archangels, may it please God to grant us the gift of perseverance in the Faith, and in all good works, that we may be thereby enabled to attain the glory of Paradise. Amen.

Our Father, Three Hail Marys

1. By the intercession of St. Michael and the heavenly choir of the Angels, may God grant us their guardianship through this mortal life, and after death a happy entrance into the everlasting glory of Heaven. Amen.

Our Father, Three Hail Marys

(Here, say on the 4 beads nearest to the medal, the Our Father prayer…one in honour of each of the following leading angels: St. Michael, St. Gabriel, St. Raphael, Our Guardian Angel)

Conclusion

O glorious prince, St. Michael, leader and commander of the heavenly host, guardian of the souls of men, conqueror of the rebel angels, steward of the palace of God, our worthy leader, endowed with holiness and power, delivers us from every evil.

With full confidence we have recourse to you, that by your gracious protection we may be enabled to make progress every day in the faithful service of God.

Pray for us, most blessed Michael,
Prince of the Church of Jesus Christ,
that we may be made worthy of His promises.

Glory be to the Father and to the Son,
and to the Holy Spirit,
As it was in the beginning,
is now, and ever shall be,
world without end. Amen.

Archangel Gabriel

Gabriel is the archangel whose name means "God is my strength". He sits on the left hand of God in heaven and is second only to Michael in the angelic hierarchy. Judaism, Christianity and Islam hold him in the same high regard. Gabriel is prominently featured in both the New Testament and the Koran. He and Michael are the only two angels identified by name in the Old Testament. In a realm of beings who bear messages from God, Gabriel has borne some of the most important. In the Gospel of Luke he announces the birth of John the Baptist to Zachariah and the birth of Jesus to the Virgin Mary. Gabriel is also the angel to consult when interpreting dreams and visions, perhaps because he has appeared in so many. Saint Gabriel's feast day is celebrated on both 18th March and 29th September. He is the patron saint of messengers, those who work for broadcasting and telecommunications such as radio, postal workers, clerics, diplomats and stamp collectors.

St. Gabriel the Archangel

St. Gabriel is a powerful messenger of God, who can assist us in our journey towards heaven as well. The prayer to the Archangel Gabriel, asks him to "intercede for us at the throne of divine mercy".

Blessed Saint Gabriel, Archangel
We beseech you to intercede for us at the throne of divine mercy:
As you announced the mystery of the Incarnation to Mary, so through
your prayers may we receive strength of faith and courage of spirit,
and thus find favour with God and redemption through Christ our Lord.
May we sing the praise of God our Saviour with the angels and saints
in heaven forever and ever
AMEN

Archangel Raphael

Archangel Raphael is known by numerous titles, including "Chief of Guardian Angels", "Regent of the Sun" and the "Angel of Science and Knowledge". The word Raphael means "God heals" and he is commonly associated with the ability to heal the sick and infirm. Raphael is in charge of healing the earth and its people. Raphael is the guardian angel and patron of travellers, especially those on pilgrimages, the blind, of meetings, of nurses, of physicians, medical workers and matchmakers. His feast day is celebrated on September 29th.

Saint Raphael the Archangel

Glorious Archangel St. Raphael,
great prince of the heavenly court,
you are illustrious for the gifts of
wisdom and grace. You are a
guide of those who journey by land

*or sea or air, consoler of the
afflicted, and refuge of sinners.
I beg you, assist me in all my
needs and in all the sufferings of
this life, as once you helped the
young Tobias on his travels.
Because you are the "medicine of
God", I humbly pray you to heal the
Many infirmities of my soul and the
Ills that afflict my body. I especially
ask of you the favour of (here name
your favour), and the great grace of
purity to prepare me to be the
temple of the Holy Spirit.*

Amen

Archangel Uriel

One of the most popular representatives of the fourth Archangel Uriel whose name means "Fire of God" – shows him holding a flame in the palm of his hand. He serves as a muse for writers and teachers. Archangel Uriel is the angel who warned Noah of the impending flood and the apocryphal scriptures identify him as the angel who governs thunderstorms. He is the patron of the arts and sciences for his ability to inspire and awaken the intellect. His feast day is celebrated on 29th September, 10th October, 18th November. He is celebrated as the patron angel of artists and intellectuals because of his work bringing beautiful thoughts to people.

Archangel Uriel

O Illustrious St. Uriel, the Archangel of God's Divine Justice, as you hold the heavenly scales that weigh our lives on earth, we ask you to intercede for us, that God may forgive us all our sins. Obtain for us the grace of true repentance & conversion of heart that we may be spared of the punishment we deserve. Offer our prayers to God in our search for true peace and happiness founded on truth & justice. We pray for those who are suffering inhumanities, dying because of injustice and the oppressed due to manipulation & exploitation. We also pray for our less fortunate brothers & ourselves for the following intentions

(Here Mention Requests)

Present to God the Father all these petitions through Jesus Christ our Lord together with the Holy Spirit forever & ever. Amen.

Archangel Jophiel

Archangel Jophiel, which means "beauty of God," is widely known as the Angel of Beauty. Jophiel is thought to work with Christine and be a companion of Archangel Metatron. When I contact Jophiel, she gives me the gift of wisdom to clearly see the beauty in all things. In tough times, this can be especially helpful.

Archangel Jophiel

I call upon you now
Help me to see the beauty in simplicity.
Remind me that beauty comes from within
Inspire me to create with God's grace.
Guide me with your divine beauty;
Motivate me with positive thoughts
Empower me with love.
Amen

53

Archangel Azrael

Archangel Azrael's name means "whom God helps." However, he is often referred to as the Angel of Death. Azrael meets souls and helps them in transition to death. In addition to helping newly crossed souls adjust, he also helps loved ones who are still on the earth plane in dealing with grief and processing their loss. Archangel Azrael helps ministers and spiritual teachers from all belief systems and religions in their spiritual counselling, and assists grief counsellors to shield themselves from absorbing their client's pain to guide their words and actions. This archangel assists in all types of transitions and endings, not just those involved in loss and death. Archangel Azrael does not act independently but is only informed by God when the time has come to take a soul.

ARCHANGEL AZRAEL

I call upon you now to stand by me.
Please surround my family as we grieve.
Pour your divine light onto us;
Healing all emotional pain and comforting us.
Remind us "We will meet again".
Bless those as they leave onto a better place.
Amen

Archangel Chamuel

Archangel Chamuel's name means "he who sees God". This Archangel has been called by many names throughout history and therefore is sometimes confused with other angels. His mission is to bring peace to the world and as such he protects the world from fear and lowers vibrating and negative energies. He is believed to have all-knowing, vision seeing the interconnectedness between all things. Archangel Chamuel assists us in finding strength and courage to face adversity when it seems we have none left. He can also find items that are lost, to find important parts of our lives such as life purpose, a love relationship, a new job and supportive friendships, and to find solutions to problems. Archangel Chamuel is the patron who helps anxiety, brings peace and repairs relationships and misunderstandings.

Archangel Chamuel

I call upon you now,
Please give me the gift of forgiveness
Please grant me inner peace,
Please create unity in my relationships,
I will believe in you I trust.
Amen

Chapter 5

Guardian Angels

Your guardian angel is the best gift you've ever been given. These angels will always look after you and are personally assigned to you for your entire life. They are standing by your side right now, pouring their love into you. They have loved you unconditionally since the time of your creation. 'The dignity of a soul is so great, that each has a guardian angel from its birth' *St. Jerome.*

Our soul knows our guardian angel. They are in constant communication with each other as they are connected through love.

Personal guardian angels are frequently the spirits of deceased loved ones whose work is detected only by the individuals they protect. Their guidance may come in the form of intuition, dreams, meaningful "signs" and coincidences. The *Hafaza* of Muslim legend, for example, are guardian angels who defend mortals against demons.

When angels of diverse faiths cannot save people from death, they will escort the departing souls on their journey to the next world. The guardian angels of Christianity belong to the choir of angels, the lowest rank of the angelic hierarchy. These angels are placed furthest away from

God but also closest to earth, which makes them perfectly situated to watch over humanity.

In Hinduism, guardian angels help people achieve close union with everyone and everything in the universe. Hindus believe in a different concept of guardian angels than found in other religions such as Judaism, Christianity and Islam.

Hinduism allows worship of many types of Gods, such as Lord Shiva, Lord Vishnu, Lord Hanuman, Sia Baba, Neem Karoli Baba, Yogananda, Swami Rama, Goddess Kali and Babaji, who act like guardian angels. Hinduism's divine beings or angels are spiritual in nature, yet often appear to people in material form, looking like human beings. The Hindu guardian angel is more like a type of God that combines two different spiritual forces. The Devas and the Atman. Devas are deities who help and guard people, pray for people and promote the spiritual growth of people and other living beings like animals and plants. Devas literally means "shining ones" and they are thought to inhabit the higher astral plane.

The Atman is a divine spark inside each person that acts as a higher self, and directs people towards higher levels of consciousness. The Atman, which represents the part of each person that lives forever despite changing through different reincarnations just as a soul does, urges people to move toward enlightenment, to understand the universe and become one within unity. Major gods, minor gods, the planets, human gurus, and ancestors may all play a protective role like that of a guardian angel during times of crisis or stress, during illness, in the face of physical danger, or when going through challenges in life.

To My Guardian Angel – Help me when I stray

Dear Angel, in His goodness God gave you to me to guide,
protect, and enlighten me,
and to bring me back to the right way when I go astray.

Encourage me when I am disheartened,
and instruct me when I err in judgement.

Help me to become more Christlike,
and so, some day to be accepted into company of the Angels
and Saints in heaven.
Amen.

Human gurus are Hindu spiritual teachers who have developed divinity inside them. Gurus are often viewed as soothsayers, and guide people through their spiritual journey in this life.

Planets like Saturn, also known as Shani, can be called on to protect believers. This planet may especially be called on for protection if it is in your horoscope. Hindus usually meditate when communicating with guardian angels, reflecting on their thoughts and sending them out into the universe rather than saying verbal prayers. Hindus practice fire and water prayers and offer fruit, milk and ghee while praying to their guardian angels for help, and in turn receive blessings from their guardian angels.

The Bhagavad Gita, Hinduism's main sacred text, refers to angelic beings as demigods or minor gods, "By this sacrifice unto the Supreme Lord the demigods are propitiated; the demigods being propitiated will mutually propitiate you and you will obtain supreme blessings" *Bhagavad Gita 3:11*

Buddhism also believes that every living thing – person, animal or plant – has an angelic being also called the deva (male) or devi (female) assigned to guard it and help it grow and prosper. Each devi and deva acts like divine energy, inspiring and motivating the person or other living thing to better understand the universe and become one with it. Everyone and everything that is alive is infused with energy from God and protected by devas.

Guardian angels can also appear in white orbs of light. If a guardian angel appears to you inside orbs, it may be simply to encourage you and remind you that you are loved and cared for. Or it may be there to inspire you to have faith when you are going through challenging circumstances. This is the angel's way of conferring a blessing to those whom they appear. Angel orbs can come in different colours and indicate the type of energy that is present within the orb.

The colours usually indicate the meanings of different angel light rays. These are:

Blue – (power, protection, faith, courage and strength)
Yellow – (wisdom for decision)
Pink – (love and peace)
White – (the purity and harmony of holiness)
Green – (healing and prosperity)
Red – (wise service)
Purple – (mercy and transformation)

In addition, orbs may feature colours beyond the seven angel light rays that are associated with other meanings, such as:

Silver - (a spiritual message)
Gold – (unconditional love)
Black – (evil)
Brown – (danger)
Orange – (forgiveness)

Occasionally, you may be able to see the faces of spirits inside angel orbs. Such faces reveal clues to the emotional messages that the angels are expressing.

You may also see a shadow of your guardian angel while you are praying or meditating. Shadows usually appear as an outline figure nearby.

Your guardian angel may also send you a visual message about what you have been considering by causing an image symbolising a certain meaning to show up for you in a vision.

Pay attention to any symbolic images that your guardian angel sends as they are clearly showing you this image for a reason. You can ask your guardian angel to clarify the meaning of images to be sure that you understand the messages they are trying to convey to you.

Also keep in mind that specific numbers, colours, shapes and shadows you see may have symbolic meaning.

Your guardian angel can also communicate with you while you are sleeping. Your angel may show you symbolic images or your angel might appear in your dreams. Usually, when your angel appears in your dreams you will recognise the angel, even if you have never seen them before. You will have a clear, deep understanding that the figure you see is your guardian angel. Your angel may appear in your dreams in human form – as a wise teacher, for example or in heavenly form with a glorious angelic appearance. Focus on enjoying the blessing of a visit from your guardian angel and deciphering the visual message your angel wants to communicate to you.

"The Divine realm extends to the earthly; but the later, illusory in nature, does not contain the essence of reality" Mahavatar Babaji.

Sometimes you may smell a distinctive fragrance, one that conveys a particular message to you. This can mean your guardian angel is contacting you. These angels often send a scent of flowers, especially roses, which have the highest energy vibration value of any flower. The scent is a sign that he or she is with you and wants to encourage you.

Other scents that symbolise angel messages:

Frankincense – spiritual enlightenment
Rose – comfort and encouragement
Grapefruit – gratitude
Mint – purity
Cinnamon – peace
Spruce – joy

Your guardian angel might send you a message through touch: when your guardian angel senses a moment when you might especially need encouragement, your angel may embrace you in a way that feels as if another person is hugging you, yet no one is visible. You might experience this hug when you are praying or meditating about something that causes you great pain, such as trauma that you have experienced.

Guardian angels work within light rays that contain electromagnetic energy. When your guardian angel is communicating with you about a matter of importance, you might sense that energy touching you, as if an electric current is flowing through your body. Though the sensation is powerful, it does not hurt you, as high voltage physical electricity would.

"Always bear this in mind: Everything is in God's hands,
and you are His tool to be used by Him as He pleases. Try to grasp the
significance of 'all is His'. and you will immediately feel free from all
burdens. What will be the result of your surrender to Him?
None will seem alien, all will be your very own Self."
Anandamayi Ma

You might also feel the physical presence of your guardian angel sitting next to you on a sofa or chair, whenever you are praying or meditating.

By sitting beside you, your guardian angel is sending you the message that he or she is listening carefully to your thoughts and feelings.

When your guardian angel touches you, you might feel the sensation of a warm rich liquid, like honey or oil, pouring over you. Your angel may touch part of your body, such as your head. This type of touch is a message meant to convey deep unconditional love.

You can strengthen your connection with your guardian angel through using crystals in your prayer or meditation. First though you must cleanse your crystal by putting it in soil or rinsing it with water. These crystals are only tools to help you better connect with angels at their frequencies. Place your trust in the source of their energy. God created these crystals for you to use. Seek God's purpose for your life, knowing that he loves you and wants only the best for you. Hold or touch your crystal so that its energy is in physical contact with your body. Begin to communicate with God's angels about your concerns. Listen to whatever message God and the angels may choose to send to you, and thank them for communicating with you.

"Thank you Guardian Angel for answering my specific prayers"

Great crystals to start with:
Rose quartz for unconditional love
Amethyst for spiritual awareness and safe travels
Turquoise for healing
Carnelian for creativity
Clear quartz for meditation
Aventurine for confidence and self-worth
Citrine for abundance
Black tourmaline for grounding

How to use your crystals:

1. Set your intention after cleansing. Speak or say mentally what you would like to receive from your special crystal. Use your intuition when deciding which way of using the crystal is best for you. You can use it during healing, around or on the body/chakras, during meditation, or near you during yoga.

2. You may use it on your altar during ceremonies. You may wish to use different types of stones for different rooms in the home, such as a protection stone in the bedroom or concentration stone in the office.

3. You may carry it around with you in your pocket or purse to have its powerful qualities close by you at all times.

4. You may use it as jewellery or put on or under your pillow.

5. Exchange. I like to give crystals that have soaked up my energy to loved ones.

Aunty Brid is my guardian angel. She died too young at the age of 47 years from breast cancer. I was only fifteen when she died and I used to stay at her house to help her while she was sick. Her death and life had a profound effect on me.

Your guardian angel is a pure spirit created by God, and exists as an individual person with an individual mind and a free will just like man. Unlike man, an angel has no body but can appear in a body when God wills, on an occasion when it may be necessary that we identify with them. This is rare but it does happen. I was 21 years of age and the year was 1997 when I saw my first vision of my Aunty Brid. I was driving along, minding my own business when a car hit me. I was fully conscious for the whole accident. I can remember my car spinning around the road and I could see the trees flashing one either side of me. One moment the road was there, wide and safe, and the next there was a loud noise and a smell of petrol, and the kind of pain that you may or may not recover from.

A car crash comes as a complete shock. I can vividly remember the car hitting a tree and then my head hitting the steering wheel. I hit it with such a belt that I must have blacked out. I had a vision of going through a tunnel and seeing a bright light, and hearing a voice saying *'go back Michelle, go back!'* I woke up from my vision only to see my Aunty Brid, my guardian angel with her two hands folded on the window of the driver's door and she told me not to worry, that I would be ok and help was on its way. Then she disappeared.

She looked just like she did when she was alive, with the same soft expression on her face. And I felt the reassurance and calmness I always felt after seeing her. Within a minute of seeing this vision, an off-duty nurse travelling from Killarney to Castleisland stopped and came over to me and asked me if I could move my legs. She immediately called the guards, the fire-brigade and the ambulance. This nurse was also an angel that God and my Aunty Brid had sent to help me.

I was cut out of the car by the fire-brigade and when everyone saw how damaged my car was, they couldn't understand how I had escaped death. Hearing this, I could not help but think back to when my aunty Brid was dying and she told me that she would never forget what I had done for her, and that she would always look after me.

Aunty Brid has looked after me on numerous occasions when I am anxious about something, and I always pray to her. When I visit her grave, she instantly connects with me. I feel her presence always around me. I have had the privilege of seeing her appear to me many times since her death. I remember when I opened up the first of the seven wells of Kingdom Water, she came to me and told me how delighted she was that I had done this. At every stage she has guided me, along with my angels. She has encouraged me to write this book and guided me every step of the way.

A MOTHER'S PRAYER

TO THE GUARDIAN ANGEL OF HER CHILDREN

I humbly salute you,
O faithful Friend of my children!
I give you heartfelt thanks for all the love and goodness you show to them.

At some future day I shall, with thanks
more worth than I can now give,
repay your care for them,
and before the whole heavenly count acknowledge their indebtedness
to your guidance and protection.

I ask you to continue to watch over them,
provide for all their needs of body and soul.
Pray, also, for me and for my whole family,
that we may all one day rejoice
in your blessed company in heaven.
Amen.

PRAYER OF THANKS TO THE FATHER FOR OUR GUARDIAN ANGELS

Heavenly Father, Your infinite love for us has chosen a blessed Angel in heaven and appointed him our guide during our earthly pilgrimage. Accept our thanks for such a great blessing. Grant that we may experience the assistance of our holy protector in all our necessities. And to you, holy, loving Angel and guide, given to us by the Father, please watch over us with all the tenderness of your angelic heart. Keep us always on the way that leads to heaven, and cease not to pray for us until we have attained our final destiny, eternal salvation. Then we shall love you for all eternity. We shall praise and glorify you unceasingly for all the good you have done for us while here on earth. Especially being a faithful and watchful protector of our children. Take our place, and supply what may be wanting in us through human frailty, short-sightedness, or sinful neglect.

Lighten, O perfect servant of God. Our heavy task. Guide our children, that they may love Jesus, and follow Him faithfully, and preserve till they attain Eternal life.

Amen

To My Guardian Angel – Help me when I stray

Dear Angel, in His goodness God gave you to me to guide,
protect, and enlighten me,
and to bring me back to the right way when I go astray.

Encourage me when I am disheartened,
and instruct me when I err in judgement.

Help me to become more Christlike,
and so, some day to be accepted into company of the Angels
and Saints in heaven.

Amen

Short Morning Prayer to your Guardian Angel

Angel of God,
my holy protector,
given to me from heaven by God for my protection,
I fervently beseech you:
enlighten me and preserve me from all evil,
instruct me in good deeds and direct me on the path of salvation.
Amen

Chapter 6

Mary Queen of Angels

Mother Mary, Our Lady of Fatima, Lourdes and Knock is the Divine Mother of Jesus. She was given the title 'Queen of Angels' because she went straight to heaven. She has a strong connection to Archangel Michael as they are both linked to the blue ray of protection and strength. From as far back as when I was four years of age, I can remember my grandmother Nora reciting the Hail Mary:

'Hail Mary Full of Grace, the Lord is with thee, blessed art thou among women and blessed is the fruit of thy womb, Jesus, Holy Mary Mother of God Pray for our sinners now and at the hour of our death Amen'

To this day it is the most powerful mantra in my toolbox of prayers, something I use for praying and meditating. For me it is the most powerful mantra of them all. I have recited thousands of 'Hail Marys' in my lifetime. Any time I have needed strength and courage during the dark days of my life – of which there have been many – the power of this mantra has pulled me through. Although Mary is closely associated with the Catholic Church, her energy is non-denominational.

Protestants share the belief that Mary is the mother of Jesus and "Blessed among women" – *Luke 1:42*, but they generally do not agree that Mary is to be venerated. They consider her to be an outstanding example of life dedicated to God but they do not accept certain church doctrines such as her being preserved from sin. Martin Luther argued about the veneration of Mary and in 1532, Luther stopped celebrating the Feast of the Assumption of Mary.

MARY QUEEN OF THE ANGELS

August Queen of Heaven!
Sovereign Mistress of the angels!
You who from the beginning as received from God the power
and mission to crush the head of Satan,
we humbly beseech you to send your Legions,
that, under your command and by your power,
they may pursue the evil spirits,
encountered them on every side,
resist their bold attacks and drive them into the
abyss of eternal woe.
Amen

In Islamic religion The Virgin Mary holds a singularly exalted place, and she is considered by the Quran to have been the greatest woman in the history of humankind. The Islamic scriptures recounts the Divine promise given to Mary as being; "Mary! God has chosen thee, and punished thee; He had chosen thee above all the women of creation" 3:42

Mary is the only woman named in the Quran and she is mentioned or referred to in the scripture a total of 50 times.

In the Catholic church the veneration of Mary, Mother of Jesus encompasses various Marian devotions which include prayers, music, poetry, the seven sorrows of the rosary and the scapular, or miraculous medal.

"It is necessary to go back to Mary if we want to return to that truth about Jesus Christ, truth about the church and truth about man".

Throughout my life I have been fortunate to have a strong connection with Our Lady. My local parish church where I was baptised is called St. Mary's. The primary school I attended in Knocknagoshel is also named after her: St. Mary's 'Scoil Mhuire'.

St. Mary gave birth to Jesus the Saviour of Humanity, so naturally she is the patroness of all humanity, and the patron saint of any good or worthwhile endeavour.

In 2010 while on a trip to Turkey I ended up visiting the ancient city of Ephesus, and the house of The Virgin Mary. This house is where Mary, Mother of Jesus, supposedly spent the last years of her life. Mary arrived at Ephesus together with St. John and lived there until her Assumption, according to both Catholic and Orthodox beliefs. Pilgrimages have been coming to the house since 1896. This house has never been officially recognised by the Catholic Church as the home of Mary, although several popes have visited the site. Pope Leo XIII blessed the house of the Virgin Mary during his pilgrimage in 1896.

In 1951 Pope Pius XII gave the house of the Virgin Mary the status of a Holy Place and a Catholic place of pilgrimage. Pope Paul VI paid a visit in July 1967. He also visited the house and granted a plenary absolution for all those who went there. In more recent history, Pope John Paul II visited in 1979 and in 2006 Pope Benedict XVI celebrated a holy mass at this place of pilgrimage. Although these papal visits have no dogmatic value, they show the religious importance of this sacred site.

When I visited this sacred site, I was greeted by a huge golden statue of the Virgin Mary on the road at the entrance to the house. For a moment at first glance, I thought I was in Ellis Island, as the statue looked so very much like the Statue of Liberty. The Virgin Mary's statue is so powerful that you cannot but feel her presence. White fluffy clouds dotted the azure blue sky as the sun beamed beautifully down, casting a golden glow over the house. It was a sign from Our Lady that she was delighted that I had taken the time to visit her house.

Beautiful olive trees adorn the sides of the way leading to Mary's house. These were apparently planted by the Lazarist Fathers in 1898. I was first greeted by a small statue of St. Anne and another statue of St. Mary. To the south-east of the house there is a rectangular atrium with a water reservoir. I could not get over how small her house – or chapel, as it is now called – was. The statue of the Virgin of Lourdes is placed on a marble altar. To the left of the altar is a storeroom and to the right of the altar is the bedroom of the Blessed Virgin, with a bunk fixed to the wall. This room is called the Quran room. The presence of Our Lady is so powerful there. As I sat and prayed, she appeared inside an orb in a golden light, swirling around several times. At first, I thought I was seeing things, but then her image grew clear. She said nothing, just appeared for two minutes. Her energy is unconditional and loving, and her presence is so peaceful.

On my journey of discovering Kingdom Water, Our Lady has appeared to me on several occasions. She appeared to me after opening the first of the seven wells on a Sunday morning and asked me to pray the Hail Mary. She kept appearing every morning for a week. The energy was so emotional and loving that every hair on my head stood up. I recited the Hail Mary and I knew that she, along with my ancestors, had gifted me Kingdom Water. I also felt that with her power behind me that there was no one going to stand in my way. With Our Lady's and Archangel Michael's protection, I knew that the healing minerals and spiritual message in this water would reach many people and bless many lives. Our Lady appeared to me on many occasions. I connected with her soul instantly each time she appeared.

Our Lady guides me on what she requests me to do and how she wants me to help people. One morning she requested that I teach meditation and advised me to set up a zoom class called 'Awaken the Divine Goddess within'. She wants me to bridge the gap between east and west. I thought she was crazy asking me to do this. I asked her 'who is going to come?', and she said "*do not worry, Michelle; I will send the people to you*" and so she has. Our Lady's request is simple: just get people to pray the 'Hail Mary'. Strangers began contacting me when they heard about Kingdom Water, and called me for samples of the water. Our Lady works through me. I am like a conduit for Our Lady; I act as a medium for her, and help people on their journeys.

Prayer to Our Lady for Assistance
Memorare Prayer

The Memorare invites us to ask the Blessed Mother for her assistance and her grace, especially when we feel most troubled in our daily lives.

Remember, O most gracious Virgin Mary, that never was it known that anyone who fled to thy protection, implored thy help, or sought thy intercession was left unaided. Inspired with this confidence, I fly to thee, O Virgin of virgins, my Mother; to thee do I come; before thee I stand, sinful and sorrowful. O Mother of the Word Incarnate, despise not my petitions, but in thy mercy hear and answer me.
Amen

Our Lady has connected with many of the people I have brought to churches. She chooses who she wants to see her and gives them a loving message. Without Our Lady's presence in my life, I honestly feel I would have not come through some of the most difficult challenges I have faced. As part of my spiritual journey with discovering Kingdom Water,

I travelled to Lourdes, Fatima, Knock and the Himalayas. Our Lady has a huge connection with all of these places. While praying at the grotto in Lourdes, I made a strong connection with Our Lady. There, I cleansed the baggage I had been carrying around possibly for most of my life. I felt a huge release of emotions. During the three days that I spent in Lourdes, I felt the similarities with Lourdes, Our Lady and Kingdom Water, and knew they were connected.

On my last day there, I asked Our Lady for her guidance with Kingdom Water and I made a promise that I would be back to visit her again in the future.

Saint Mary, the Blessed Virgin Mother of God, and Queen of Heaven is the greatest and holiest among all saints. Mother Mary has many names. St. Mary is also known as Our Lady of Sorrows, Our Lady of Perpetual Help, Our Lady of Good Courage, Our Lady of Navigators, Our Lady Undoer of Knots and Our Lady Madonna in medieval Italian. St. Mary carried and gave birth to the saviour of humanity, so she is patroness of all humanity. Our Lady is the patron saint of any good or worthwhile endeavour.

I went for a bath at the grotto and prayed to Our Lady for help and guidance with Kingdom Water.

O Most Holy Virgin

Do not – in the midst of thy greatness – forget our earthly sorrows.
Cast down thy tender look upon those who suffer, who struggle against
difficulties and who cease not wetting their lips in the bitter draughts of
this life' Have pity – I beseech thee- on those who, although united in love,
have been cruelly parted, and take pity on the lonely-hearted. Grant us
thy help in our unbelief, and have compassion on those most dear to us.
Compassionate those who mourn, who pray, who tremble, and grant all
Hope and Peace.

My God, I believe, I adore, I hope and I love You!
I ask pardon of You for those who do not believe, do not adore,
do not hope and do not love You. Most Holy Trinity, Father, Son and
Holy Spirit, I adore You profoundly, and I offer You the most precious
Body, Blood, Soul and Divinity of Jesus Christ, present in all the
tabernacles of the world, in reparation for the outrages, sacrileges and
indifference with which He Himself is offended.
and, through the infinite merits of His most Sacred Heart,
and the Immaculate Heart of Mary, I beg of You the conversion
of poor sinners.

I needed to buy a suitcase to bring back bottles of water, so I walked through the back streets of Lourdes, away from all the commercial shops and I saw a lovely old shop called Atelier Marie. The shopkeeper, Collette, had a fabulous collection of Archangel Michael's prayers and I bought some.

That was when I got talking to Collette, and she said that she was reading a book on Saint Michael called Archangel Parle en Sicile. The author of the book had dropped her a copy of it only yesterday.

For some reason, I began to tell her about Archangel Michael and my water. She said Archangel Michael was making this happen. She sold me a copy of the book she was reading, and told me I needed to meet the man who Archangel Michael appeared to in Italy. She said that her shop is off the beaten track, and that when a customer walks into her shop she always believes it is Our Lady who sent them. I walked away from her shop certain that this was another sign from Archangel Michael.

When I went to Lourdes for my three-day trip, it was my third trip there. I have always felt a strong connection, ever since our parish put on a production of *Massabielle, The Story of Lourdes* back in 1987, in which I played the role of Bernadette's sister. Since then, Lourdes has held a special place in my heart.

For me, Lourdes is all about the grotto and Our Lady, and on that third trip, I spent the whole day of the first day praying at the grotto. I actually cried most of the day. I felt a release of emotions and cleansed the baggage that I had been carrying around, possibly for most of my life. It was such a relief.

I saw water spirits and angels in the grotto and could feel their presence. I could not help thinking of the similarities between Kingdom Water and Lourdes water.

Lourdes is situated in the foothills of the Pyrenees and Talbots Bridge is situated in the foothills of Knocknagoshel.

Bernadette was gifted Lourdes water by Our Lady, and I was gifted Kingdom Water by the angels. Most importantly, Bernadette was just an ordinary person, like me.

Prayer to Our Lady of Lourdes

O Holy Virgin,
in the midst of your days of glory, do not forget the sorrows of this earth.
Cast a merciful glance upon those who are suffering, struggling against
difficulties, with their lips constantly pressed against life's bitter cup.
Have pity on those who love each other and are separated.
Have pity on our rebellious hearts.
Have pity on our weak faith.
Have pity on those who weep, on those who pray, on those who fear.
Grant hope and peace to all.
Amen

Two weeks after my trip to Lourdes, I drove to Dublin airport again for a trip to Fatima.

Just a few miles from the airport, while on the motorway, I saw four huge 20ft angels in the sky, one with a trumpet. I took this as a sign they were watching and guiding me on my journey to Fatima, and that there was a message waiting for me there. Then as I drove, in the sky in front of me I saw a vision of 50 or more rocks, with minerals dropping down from the sky. At first, I thought, "my God, I could crash the car" but deep down I understood there was a strong and powerful message there.

I rang my spiritual adviser, Guruji Shashi in India, from the airport and told him what had happened. He told me to phone again when I arrived in Fatima.

I called my Guruji again from the bus on the way up to Fatima and he said to head straight to the main square, and phone him when I got there, which I did. Shashi asked how I was and I said I felt great, at peace with myself. I could just feel the energy of Fatima within me. He told me that I needed to go and pray for an hour, and to call him back when I had done that.

I prayed at the chapel of the Apparitions. I asked Our Lady of Fatima for guidance. After that, I phoned my Guruji and he said to pray for another hour and then phone him.

I walked up to the Basilica on the eastern side and I knelt down in front of the tomb of Francisco Marto, one of the three shepherd children to whom Our Lady appeared. I prayed the rosary. I cannot describe the feeling inside, but something told me that a miracle was about to happen. I went over to the other tombs – Lucia of Jesus and Jacinta Marto – and said the rosary. I sat in the Basilica and asked all three, along with Our Lady of Fatima, for guidance on the water.

I prayed for about an hour and a half and then realised I must call my Guruji Shashi. I went outside and sat down on a wall to make the call. He asked me how I was now and I said I was really at peace and something beautiful had happened to me in front of Francisco Marto's tomb. I said I was humbled to be there at the feast of Our Lady of Fatima. My Guruji then put me on to Dr. Praful, an Indian consultant working with me on

Kingdom Water, who said he had been doing his own research and that we needed to trademark Kingdom Water. I told him I would do that, and that I needed to register the domain name.

Dr. Praful said he wanted to devise a plan that was fair to everyone as to how the company would be divided into shares. He told me that he was looking at many different products we could use our base water for, incorporating the medicinal value, and that he was in talks with multinationals such as Coca Cola & Pepsi, and that we would be delivering a premium product to the world. I told him the results of the water analysis would be back within a few days, and we agreed to talk then as Dr. Praful wanted to put a final proposal to the Indian company who were planning to invest in Kingdom Water, one that we would all be happy with. Clearly, Dr. Praful meant business. I felt then that whatever prayers I had said in the Basilica, Our Lady of Fatima was helping me. That night I spoke to my Guruji and he said 'before you get the bus back to the airport in the morning, go down to the square and make a promise to Our Lady of Fatima that you will be back to do the full rounds of Fatima.' I said I would.

The following morning, I woke at 5am and there over my bed were angels sending me more telepathic messages. I watched this for half an hour and then realised I had to shower and get down to the square.

Something told me that I needed to go back up to the Basilica and pray again in front of Francisco Marto's grave. It was 5.40am by then, and still dark outside. I borrowed a bike from the hotel, for speed, and cycled down to the square and prayed in front of the chapel of Apparitions. I cycled up to the eastern side of the Basilica to Francisco Marto's tomb and kneeled down.

I said a Novena to Our Lady. As I got up, an angel whispered in my ear to kneel back down and say the Memorare prayer. So I did.

I have undying faith in the power of "The Hail Mary" mantra. For me, this is the most powerful mantra ever. I also like to pray the Memorare prayer to ask Our Lady for assistance and grace, this is especially beneficial when we feel most troubled in our daily lives.

So I kneeled down, closed my eyes and said the Memorare to Our Lady of Fatima:

Remember, O most gracious Virgin Mary,
that never was it known that anyone who fled to thy protection,
implored thy help, or sought thy intercession was left unaided.
Inspired with this confidence, I fly to thee, O Virgin of virgins, my Mother;
to thee do I come; before thee I stand, sinful and sorrowful.
O Mother of the Word Incarnate, despise not my petitions,
but in thy mercy hear and answer me.
Amen

I opened my eyes and there was the same angel sign on Francisco Marto's tomb that I had seen an hour earlier on the ceiling in my hotel room. I shed a silent tear and looked up to heaven and thanked Our Lady of Fatima, because I knew there was my answer. A miracle had taken place in Fatima, right before my eyes.

I promised Our Lady that I would be back to do the full rounds. I took a sample of the water from the fountain, and then I left, with the most profound feeling of relief and inner happiness. I knew that the Kingdom Water mission was about to be accomplished, thanks to Our Lady of Fatima on her feast day.

Fatima Prayer

"Oh Jesus forgive us our sins, save us from the fire of hell. Lead all souls to Heaven, especially those most need of your mercy."

When I look back now over my years – everywhere I have travelled, I have always ended up in a church dedicated to Our Lady.

I remember on a buying trip for my interior design business, Mibeau Interiors, I ended up in Milan and visited The Metropolitan Cathedral – Basilica of the Nativity of Saint Mary. The Cathedral took nearly six centuries to complete. It is the largest church in Italy, larger than St. Peter's Basilica in the State of Vatican City. On entering the Basilica one cannot but feel the presence of Our Lady in this sacred place. The size of the stained-glass windows in the Basilica must be, I reckon, the largest in the world, spanning 68ft tall and 28ft wide.

Because illiteracy was widespread back when the cathedral was constructed, stained glass windows could be used as a means of telling biblical stories, depicting episodes from the Bible and portraying the Bible authors. The stained-glass windows in the Basilica aren't just beautiful works of art through which rays of light shine, brilliantly displaying an array of colours across the pews throughout the cathedral – they also teach us about our past church history.

I happened to spend Christmas in Sydney fifteen years ago and was fortunate to attend Christmas Day Mass in St. Mary's Cathedral. It is the site of the first catholic chapel in Australia, constructed in local sandstone. The gothic revival style of its architecture is reminiscent of the great medieval cathedrals of Europe. The main aspect of the cathedral that visitors are attracted to is the crypt, located beneath the nave. This is the last resting place of the deceased Archbishops of Sydney, and is notable for the beautiful terrazzo mosaic floor, depicting the story of the creation, and symbolic titles of the Blessed Virgin Mary. It was beautiful to attend Christmas Day Mass in this sacred cathedral. Every Irish person who was there that day was interviewed by the Irish tv network, RTE, who recorded the mass. It was a beautiful experience and another message that Our Lady was minding me on my travels.

Everyone knows that Los Angeles is known as the 'City of Angels', but few know that the name is a shortened form of the original city name. The original name in English is 'City of Our Lady the Queen of Angels of the Little Portion'. I was fortunate to visit the cathedral of Our Lady of the Angels to view the tapestries created by artist John Nava. These tapestries are truly a work of art and are part of the movement that links the Renaissance medieval periods with contemporary tapestries as an art form combining great size with intricate details. The sight of these tapestries touches the soul of anyone who is privileged to see them.

We in Ireland have a huge affiliation with Our Lady. She appeared to fifteen people in Knock on the 21st August 1879. Knock was recognised as an International Shrine on March 19th 2021, after Pope Francis paid a visit to the site in 2018.

You cannot travel far in Ireland without coming across statues by the side of roads. These are dotted all around the countryside, and are Marian Shrines or just simple grottos to Our Lady.

They vary from a small statue set into a wall to large, elaborately constructed, tableaux and are often decked with fresh flowers. Many are close to holy wells, places now associated with Christian saints whose origins almost certainly date back to Pagan times, and others are situated in places that have significance locally that long predates the shrines themselves. The year 1954 was dedicated by the Vatican as a Marian year, a year of celebration of devotion to Mary. No other country embraced this year with greater fervour than Ireland. As well as erecting hundreds of shrines, commemorative stamps were issued and a majority of girls born in Ireland that year were named Marian or Mary.

Throughout the world, the church celebrates the birth of Our Lady Blessed Virgin on 8th September, because of the importance of Mary's role as the mother of Jesus. Other important dates in the life of Our Lady that people celebrate throughout the world are:

2nd February – The Presentation of Christ in the Temple, also called the purification and thanksgiving sacrifice, conducted forty days after the birth of a child. Mary fulfilled this law when she and Joseph presented Jesus in the temple.

5th March – The Annunciation of Our Lord to the Blessed Virgin Mary is celebrated on this day. The church commemorates the choice of Mary to be the saviour's mother. This message was conveyed to Mary by the Angel Gabriel, and she humbly accepted her role.

31st May – The Visitation of the Blessed Virgin Mary commemorates the visit of Mary to her cousin Elizabeth. The Gospel reading includes Mary's song The Magnificat. The Magnificat is appointed for daily use in the Church of Ireland.

According to tradition, it was Archangel Michael who led the Virgin Mary to heaven during her Assumption. He was the principal angel in charge of leading the body and soul of Mary into heaven.

There is no teaching in the Bible on Mary's death, so everything we know about this comes from apocryphal narratives. One of the most popular versions of the details of Mary's death is an early story by Bishop John of Thessalonica. In this story, an angel tells Mary that she will die in three days. She then summons relatives and friends to stay with her for two nights and they sing instead of mourning. Three days after her funeral, the Apostles – just as they did with Jesus – opened her Sarcophagus, only to find that she had been taken away by Christ.

As I have said, Mary Mother of Jesus is worshipped by Muslims as well as by Christians. On 14th June 2017, Sheikh Mohammed bin Azyed Al Nahyan, the Crown Prince of the Emirate of Abu Dhabi, decided to rename the mosque in Abu Dhabi to Mary Mother of Jesus Mosque, in a bid to consolidate bonds of humanity between followers of different religions. I was fortunate to visit this mosque in 2015. Using the name Mother Mary on this mosque was a very symbolic gesture of love and peace that we hope will be followed around the world.

In 2019 I visited Santa Maria del Mar Cathedral in Barcelona. This translates to "Saint Mary of the Sea". I decided to take a guided tour of the church. It is the most beautiful Gothic church in Barcelona, built in the heart of the medieval city located along Mediterranean shores.

Santa Maria del Mar is not actually a cathedral but people began calling it 'Cathedral of the Sea' as this Catholic church was built for the people, and financed by port workers living in the neighbourhood.

Many people look for tours of this church inspired by the best-selling novel 'La Catedral del Mar' by Ildefonso Falcones, which tells the story of a feudal conflict set around the construction of this beautiful church. After the 1428 earthquake, the stained glass which represents the coronation of the Virgin Mary was restored. In the second circle of the stained glass are symbols of the four evangelists; in the third are apostles, and in the rest are ships, saints, bishops and figures of musician angels.

The colour blue stands out above all the others as it is white glass. While I was looking at these beautiful stained-glass windows, one window in particular really stood out. It depicted the Virgin with the child and Saint Michael in the middle window of the Chapel Sant Pere. I felt Archangel Michael's presence along with Our Lady while looking at this stained-glass window. On that trip, I was in Barcelona to meet a lithium expert in relation to the healing minerals in Kingdom Water.

While visiting Italy on an interior design trip in 2003 I ended up visiting the Holy House of Mary in Loreto in Italy. Catholics pilgrims have flocked to the Holy House of Loreto since the 14th Century, to stand inside the walls where tradition holds the Virgin Mary was born, raised and greeted by the Angel Gabriel.

This Holy House is now preserved inside a Basilica in the small town of Loreto. There is a story that angels carried the Holy House from Palestine to Italy. Tradition holds that the Holy House arrived in Loreto on December 10th 1294 after a miraculous rescue from the Holy Land when the crusaders were driven out of Palestine at the end of the 13th Century.

Excavations in both Nazareth and Loreto found that similar materials are present at both sites. Archaeologists also confirmed a tradition of Loreto that third-century Christians had transformed Mary's house in Nazareth into a place of worship by building a synagogue style church around the house. A 7th Century Bishop who travelled to Nazareth noted a church built at the house where the annunciation took place.

In 1993 St. John Paul II called the Holy House of Loreto the 'Foremost shrine of international importance dedicated to the Blessed Virgin in 1993'.

Christopher Columbus made a vow to the Madonna of Loreto in 1493 when he and his crew were caught in a storm during their return journey from the Americas. He later sent a sailor to Loreto on a pilgrimage of thanksgiving on behalf of the entire crew.

Napoleon plundered the shrine and its treasury on February 13th 1797, taking with him precious jewels and other gifts offered to the Virgin Mary by European aristocracy, including several French monarchs over the centuries. Yet, the object of real value in the eyes of pilgrims, the Holy House of Mary, was left unharmed. In a homily in 1995, Saint Pope John Paul II called the Holy House of Loreto 'The house of all Gods' adopted children'.

When you visit Loreto, the actual Holy house is encased in marble at the centre of the Basilica. It is 31 feet long by 13 feet wide and, unlike many other shrines, is under the direct authority and protection of the Pope. Standing in this sacred place where Mary's fiat actually occurred is an experience beyond description. I was fortunate to join a group to receive mass in the Basilica facing the Holy House, and received many blessings from the beautiful devotion. I headed back by train to Bologna – the train station is only a short walk, about a mile, from the shrine.

I took a train from Bologna to Florence and then onto Pisa to visit the Pisa Cathedral. The Pisa Cathedral is a medieval Roman Catholic cathedral dedicated to the Assumption of the Virgin Mary. When you enter the cathedral, you are greeted by the most magnificent artworks of Mary, the Madonna and a large mosaic in the apse of Christ enthroned between the Virgin and Saint John is just beautiful. It even survived a devastating fire in 1959. There is a beautiful fresco of Mary and Child in the triumphal arch near the pulpit, with a low hanging bronze lamp that, according to a popular story, is the very lamp Galileo was watching sway gently during mass when the law of the pendulum occurred to him.

Bronze angels flank the entrance to the choir. The leaning tower is at the entrance to the Duomo and this is home to the original bronze door of San Ranieri, cast by Bonnano Pisano in 1880 while he was working at the tower.

I remember my first trip to New York, back in 1997 and my impressions of St. Patrick's Cathedral. This has become a meeting place for immigrants, tourists, Catholics, Christians and all people since its construction. It has become one of the most widely known and visited churches and landmarks of Manhattan. The highlight, for me, was the Lady Chapel dedicated to the Blessed Virgin Mary, which serves as a smaller, more private prayer space for small congregations. In the Lady Chapel, the Blessed Sacrament – the real presence of God – is reposed for adoration and prayer by the faithful. The walls are adorned by some of the most beautiful stained-glass windows, representing each mystery of the Holy Rosary, a prayerful meditation on the life of Jesus Christ and Mary the Blessed Virgin.

Our Lady Mother Mary and St. Patrick have a lot in common. St. Patrick is credited with bringing Christianity to parts of Ireland and Our Lady appeared in Knock in Ireland in 1879 along with St. Joseph and St. John the Evangelist.

Since St. Patrick baptised Christians converts over 1500 years ago, St. Patrick's Cathedral in Dublin has been a holy site and place of spiritual encounter for countless generations. It is the national cathedral of the Church of Ireland. The Lady Chapel of the cathedral was dedicated to the Blessed Virgin Mary in 1270 and now serves as a private chapel space. Today, the majority of the midweek services in the cathedral take place here.

In 2012 the St Patrick's Cathedral Lady Chapel was closed for a major conservation and cleaning project which cost €700,000. Inside the Lady Chapel is a chair which is said to have been used by King William III at a service of celebration for his victory at the Battle of the Boyne.

While on holidays in Paris I visited the Our Lady of Paris Notre Dame Basilica. I had not intended to visit this Basilica. It just appeared on my path out of nowhere. I remember going inside to light a candle and say a quiet prayer. This landmark is located in the heart of Paris, and has one of the longest and richest histories of any French cathedral. This is the site of royal weddings, the coronation of Napoleon Bonaparte as emperor and the beatification of Joan of Arc. The purpose of it being built – besides the dedication to the Virgin Mary – was for it to be an education centre. In 1345 a statute of Our Lady was fashioned and installed in place.

Notre-Dame Cathedral suffered damage and deterioration through the centuries. After the French Revolution it was rescued from possible destruction by Napoleon, who crowned himself Emperor of the French in the cathedral in 1804. Napoleon was not irreligious in the ordinary sense of the word. As a Christian and a Catholic, he recognised in religion the higher right to govern human societies. Napoleon paved his own success. Aside from being triumphant in battles and building an empire, Napoleon also laid the foundation for modern French education and created laws known as the Napoleonic code, based on common sense and equality. He was an extremely ambitious and intelligent man, known for his ability to multitask. He once said 'a society without religion is like a vessel without a compass'

Napoleon defined the status of the Roman Catholic Church in France in 1801 by signing a concordat – an agreement with the Pope – whereby he pragmatically recognised Catholicism as the religion of the 'great majority of French citizens'. This was a clever formula that was both a statement of fact, and left room for other faiths. In return, the Pope accepted many of the reforms brought about by the French Revolution, and Notre Dame was returned to the church in April 1802. In February 1821 while detained at Saint Helena Island, Napoleon's health began to deteriorate rapidly. He reconciled with the Catholic Church, and died on 5th May 1821 after receiving the sacraments of confession, extreme function and viaticum in the presence of Father Ange Vignali.

OUR LADY OF SORROWS

Father,

As your Son was raised on the Cross,
His mother Mary stood by him, sharing his sufferings.
May your Church be united with Christ
in his suffering and death
and so come to share in his rising to new life,
where he lives and reigns with you and the Holy Spirit,
and God, for ever and ever.
Amen

Two weeks after arriving back from Fatima, I got a calling to visit Knock shrine. I decided to go on a Sunday because every Sunday they have a rosary pilgrimage, followed by a beautiful mass. Knock Shrine is located in Co. Mayo in the west of Ireland. The sanctuary of Our Lady of Knock is where an apparition of the Blessed Virgin Mary, Saint Joseph, Saint John the Evangelist, an angel and Jesus Christ (the Lamb of God) appeared on the evening of Thursday 21st August 1879.

The story of Knock is very powerful. It was about 8pm on a wet blustery night when a local girl, Mary Byrne, from the village, was accompanying the priest's housekeeper, Mary McLoughlin, home. She stopped suddenly when she came in sight of the gable of the little church of Saint John the Baptist. There she saw, standing a little out from the gable, three life-sized figures. She ran home to tell her parents and soon others from the village gathered.

Witnesses stated that they saw an apparition of Our Lady, Saint Joseph and Saint John the Evangelist. Behind them and a little to the left was a plain altar and on the altar was a cross and a lamb (a traditional Catholic image of Jesus), with adoring angels. For nearly two hours, the group of 25 people stood and gazed at the figures while rain lashed them in the darkness.

For believing Catholics, the apparition held great significance. Though it was a major Irish pilgrimage site for over 100 years, Knock really established itself as a world religious site during the last quarter of the 20th century, due to the work of its long-time parish priest, Monsignor James Horan who presided over a major rebuilding of the site, including a large new Basilica alongside the old church.

Knock is famous for many cures; those who believe they are cured leave their crutches and sticks at the spot where the apparition is believed to have occurred. Many famous people, including Mother Teresa of Calcutta, have visited the site. She came in 1993. Pope John Paul II visited on September 30th 1979, to commemorate the centenary of the apparition.

On the 26th August 2018, Pope Francis visited the shrine as part of a state visit to Ireland for the Ninth World Meeting of Families.

On arrival at Knock, I visited the Apparition Chapel, as this is where I feel the presence of Our Lady. The chapel was full of people. But when one lives in harmony with oneself while recognising a vital connection to the world, one can have a quiet mind, and live contentedly no matter what.

In the chapel, I prayed the Novena to Our Lady of Knock:

Give praise to the Father almighty,
To his Son, Jesus Christ, the Lord,
To the Spirit who dwells in our hearts
Both now and forever.

Prayer to Our Lady of Knock

Our Lady of Knock, Queen of Ireland,
you gave hope to our people in a time of distress
and comforted them in sorrow.
You have inspired countless pilgrims
to pray with confidence to your divine Son,
remembering His promise:
'Ask and you shall receive, seek and you shall find';
Help me to remember that we are all pilgrims
on the road to heaven.
Fill me with love and concern for my brothers and
in Christ, especially those who live with me.
Comfort me when I am sick or lonely or depressed.
Teach me how to take part ever more reverently
in the holy Mass.

Give me a greater love of Jesus
In the Blessed Sacrament.
Pray for me now, and at the hour of my death.
Amen.

I could see many orbs and angels flying behind the altar and tears began to flood my face. It is at times like this that my tears keep my soul alive in the furnace of pain. I felt I was crying for the 25 people who witnessed the apparition on that wet evening in 1879. I could feel their presence with me as I prayed. At times like this, crying seems the smartest thing to do.

It was wet outside, and as I prayed, I could see divine presence at the gable wall and could feel the presence of Our Lady. I must have spent four hours praying, before I began my four-hour journey back home on my own. I filled a bottle with Knock holy water as I felt I needed to bless my own site where the wells were. I remember driving home to Kerry thinking how blessed I was to have the blessings of Lourdes, Fatima and now Knock helping me on my spiritual journey. It felt like another piece of the jigsaw.

When I arrived home late that night, I lit a candle on my well and blessed the well with the water from Knock. As I did so, I looked up and I saw a massive angel standing over the first of the seven springs, guarding me. There I was, four hours from Knock, blessing my land in Knocknagoshel with this very powerful water and asking our Lady of Knock to bless me on my journey with Kingdom Water.

PRAYER TO OUR LADY OF PERPETUAL HELP

Mother of Perpetual Help,
with the greatest confidence
we come before your holy picture
to be inspired by the example of your life.
We think of you at that moment when,

full of faith and trust,
you accepted God's call
to be the mother of his Son.
Help us, your children,
to accept with joy our own calling in life.
When you learned that your cousin Elizabeth was in need
you immediately went to serve her
and offer your help.
Help us, like you,
to be concerned for others.
We think of you, Mother,
at the foot of the cross.
Your heart must have bled
to see your Son in agony.
But your joy was great
when he rose from the dead,
victorious over the powers of evil.
Mother of Sorrows,
help us through the trials and
disappointments of life.
Help us not to lose heart.
May we share with you and your Son
the joy of having courageously
faced up to all the challenges of life.
Amen

Throughout my life, no matter where I have travelled in the world, my connection with Our Lady has always been so powerful, and had guided my footsteps and my curiosity.

Chapter 7

Angels in The White House

The first US President, George Washington (1732-99) had a vision of his country's future in which an angel spoke to him and revealed the destiny of the United States. George Washington told of an angel who revealed a prophetic vision of America to him at Valley Forge, where he had resolved to pass the winter of 1777. He was a very spiritual man. He was known to pray to God in secret for aid and comfort.

After George Washington's death, the writer Charles Wesley Alexander created an artistic impression of this vision, and published it as Washington's Vision.

The story goes that one afternoon in Valley Forge, Washington was preparing a dispatch when something disturbed him. He looked up and beheld standing opposite him, a singularly beautiful being. So astonished was he – for he had given strict orders not to be disturbed – that it was some moments before he found language to enquire about the cause of the visit. He asked a second, a third and even a fourth time, repeating the same question, but he received no answer from this mysterious visitor, except a slight raising of the eyebrows.

George Washington described later how he felt a strange sensation spreading through him that vibrated inside of him, but the riveted gaze of the being before him rendered volition impossible. He tried to speak but his tongue became useless, as though he had become paralysed. All he could do was to gaze steadily, vacantly at his unknown visitor. Gradually the surrounding atmosphere seemed to become filled with sensations and grew luminous. He felt like he was dying. He did not think or did not reason, he did not move; all were alike impossible in the moment. He could only consciously gaze fixedly and vacantly at his new companion. Then he heard a voice saying 'Son of the Republic, look and learn' while at the same time his visitor extended an arm eastwardly. He beheld a heavy vapor at some distance rising.

This gradually dissipated, and he recalls that he looked out upon a strange scene. Before him lay spread out in one vast plain all the countries of the world, Europe, Asia, Africa and America. He saw rolling and tossing between Europe and America the billows of the Atlantic Ocean, and between Asia and America lay the Pacific.

'Son of the Republic' said the same mysterious voice as before, 'Look and learn'. At that moment he beheld a dark, shadowy being as an angel standing or rather floating in mid-air between Europe and America. Dipping water out of the ocean in the hollow of his hand, he cast some on Europe. Immediately clouds rose from these countries and joined in the mid-ocean. For a while the cloud remained stationary and then moved slowly westward until it enveloped America in its murky folds. Sharp flashes of lighting gleamed through it at intervals and he heard the smothered groans and cries of the American people.

A second time the angel dipped water from the ocean and sprinkled it out as before. The dark cloud was drawn back to the ocean, in whose bellows it sank from view. A third time Washington heard the mysterious voice saying ' Son of the Republic, look and learn'. He then cast his eyes upon America and beheld villages and towns and cities spring up one after another, until the whole land from the Atlantic to the Pacific was dotted with them. Again he heard the mysterious voice say 'Son of the Republic, the end of the Century cometh; look and learn.' The scene instantly began to fade and dissolve and at last he saw nothing but the rising, curling vapor he had first beheld. This also disappeared and he found himself gazing upon the mysterious visitor, who in the same voice had heard before said, 'Son of the Republic, what you have seen is thus interpreted.'

'Three great perils will come upon the Republic,' he was told. 'The most fearful is the third, but in this greatest conflict the whole world united shall not prevail against her. Let every child of the Republic learn to live for his God, his land and the Union.' With these words the vision vanished and he started from his seat and felt that he had seen a vision wherein had been shown the birth, progress and destiny of the United States.

This vision became known as 'Washington's Vision'.

Washington has been painted in different lights, ranging from a deist (this is the philosophical position that rejects revelation as a source of religious knowledge and asserts that reason and observation of the natural world are sufficient to establish the existence of a Supreme Being or creator) to a believing Christian. No matter what precise conclusion is obtained there are common facts surrounding Washington's relationship with religion. He was a devout member of the Anglican church. Washington's church attendance varied throughout his life, becoming sporadic for periods of time and then picking up again during his presidency. In regards to his spirituality, Washington was generally private about his religious life. He is reported to have had regular prayer sessions in the White House and personal prayer was a large part of his life.

One well known report stated that Washington's nephew witnessed him doing personal devotions with an open Bible while kneeling in both morning and evening. It is clear that when it came to religion, George Washington was a private man, more so than with other aspects of his life. It is also clear that George Washington was a humanitarian. He helped to care for the poor and believed strongly in charity which he exercised privately.

George Washington did see God as guiding the creation of the United States. He felt he needed to discern the will of providence. These facts point to belief in a God who is hidden from humanity, yet continually influencing the events of the Universe.

Abraham Lincoln became the United States 16th President in 1861. In his first inaugural address on Monday 4th March 1861 he said, 'We are not enemies, but friends. We must not be enemies. Though passion may have strained, it must not break out bonds of affection. The mystic chords of memory will swell when again touched, as surely they will be, by the better angels of our nature'.

This was a deeply invoked and deeply personal message in the challenging times that the people of America faced then. Abraham Lincoln's speech appealed to the best instincts of human spirit as a better way to navigate through the Civil War that lay ahead. Abraham Lincoln spoke across the years. Words matter. In the difficult days ahead in all our lives, we need to hear his appeal to 'the better angels of our nature', as the better way to redefine American unity at this difficult time.

In moments of crisis, Lincoln became a kind of guardian angel to Americans, not unlike the phrase with which he closed out his inaugural address in 1861. Given the 'guardian angel' by his advisor, the New York Senator William Seward, he improved it to 'better angel'

Abraham Lincoln still speaks to us, unlike so many Presidents. His moral compass worked; he was elected at a time when no one in their right mind would have wanted the job.

Despite constant hatred from his enemies, Lincoln fought to unite Americans, and in doing so he restored a measure of racial justice. He reminded Americans that their words mattered. That helped the country to live up to its ideals, as expressed in the Declaration of Independence. Abraham Lincoln grew up in a highly religious Baptist family. He never joined any church and was a sceptic as a young man.

His mother's death had a profound effect on him. She died when Lincoln was just nine years old, and the famous words he uttered later about his mother, Nancy – 'All that I am, or hope to be, I owe to my angel mother' – simply meant 'my mom has always been there and always put us first.' Nancy Lincoln had instilled the virtues of honesty and compassion in her son and sowed the seeds of his intellectual curiosity. When his father remarried Sarah Bush Johnson, they forged a loving stepmother and stepson bond. In 1861 Lincoln confided to a relative that his stepmother had been his best friend in this world and that no son could love a mother more than he loved her.

Lincoln frequently referred to God and had a deep knowledge of the Bible, often quoting it. He believed in God, but some said he doubted the idea that Christ is God. He once wrote that the idea that Christ is God, or equal to the creator, had better be taken for granted, for by the test of reason all might become infidels on that subject, for evidence of Christ's divinity came to us in somewhat doubtful shape but that the system of Christianity was an ingenious one at least and perhaps was calculated to do good.

During the White House years, Lincoln and his family often attended the New York Avenue Presbyterian Church, where the family pew he rented is marked by a plaque. In 1862 and 1863, during the most difficult days of the Civil War and his presidency, Lincoln's utterances were sometimes marked with spiritual overtones. On Thursday February 20th 1862 at 5pm, Lincoln's eleven-year-old son William Wallace Lincoln died, possibly of typhoid fever, at the White House. This may have been the most difficult personal crisis in Lincoln's life. After the funeral, he attempted to return to his routine but was unable. One week after the funeral, he isolated himself in his office and wept all day. Several friends of Lincoln later said that his feelings about religion changed at this time. Willie had apparently often remarked that he wanted to become a minister; when his son died Lincoln reportedly said '*May God live in all. He was too good for this earth, the Good Lord has called him home, I know that he is much better in heaven*'

Spiritualism, very much in vogue at this era, was attempted by Lincoln's wife, Mary. She used the services of mediums and spiritualists to try to contact their dead son, and Lincoln allegedly attended at least one séance at the White House with his wife. He wanted to connect with his son Willie's soul.

When Bishop Matthew Simpson gave the address at Lincoln's funeral, he quoted him asking a soldier 'Do you ever find yourself talking with the dead? Since Willie's death, I catch myself every day, involuntarily talking with him as if he were with me.' At this time, the war was not going well for the Union and Lincoln was preparing to issue the preliminary Emancipation Proclamation. Lincoln sat down in his office and penned the following words;

'The will of God prevails. In great contests each party claims to act in accordance with the will of God, both *may* be and one *must* be wrong. God cannot be for and against the same thing at the same time. In the present Civil War it is quite possible that God's purpose is something different from the purpose of either party – and yet the human instrumentalities, working just as they do, are the best adaptation to effect His purpose. I am almost ready to say that this is probably true – that God wills this contest, and wills that it shall not end yet. By his mere great power, in the minds of the now contestants he could have either saved or destroyed the Union without a human contest. Yet the contest began. And having begun He could give the final victory to either side any day. Yet the contest proceeds.'

This concept continued to dominate Lincoln's public remarks for the rest of the war. In December 1863 Lincoln's secretary of the Treasury decided on a new motto: 'In God we Trust', to be engraved on US coins. Lincoln's involvement in this decision is unclear. A pious Minister told Lincoln he 'hoped the Lord is on our side', to which the President responded 'I am not at all concerned about that but it is my constant anxiety and prayer that I and this nation should be on the Lord's side'.

In 1864 some former slaves in Maryland presented Lincoln with a gift of a Bible. Lincoln responded by saying 'In regard to this great book I have but to say, it is the best gift God has given to man. All the good the Saviour gave to the world was communicated through this book. But for it, we could not know right from wrong. All things most desirable for man's welfare, here and hereafter, are to be found portrayed in it.'

In September 1864 Lincoln placed the Civil War squarely within a divine province in writing a letter to a friend, Mrs Eliza Gurney.

'The purposes of the Almighty are perfect, and must prevail, though we erring mortals may fail to accurately perceive them in advance. We hoped for a happy termination of this terrible war long before this; but God knows best and has ruled otherwise. We shall yet acknowledge His wisdom and our own errors therein. Meanwhile we must work earnestly in the best light He gives us, trusting that working still leads to the great ends He ordains. Surely He intends some great good to follow this mighty convulsion, which no mortal could make, and no mortal could stay.'

On the day Lincoln was assassinated at Ford's Theatre – April 14th 1865 – he reportedly told his wife that he wanted to visit the Holy Land and that 'there was no place he so much desired to see as Jerusalem'. On the day he was shot, Lincoln told his bodyguard Ward Hill Lamon that he had a vision from his angels that he would be assassinated. For a few days before his assassination, Lincoln shared a recent dream with a small group that included his wife. In it he walked into the East room of the White House to find a covered corpse guarded by soldiers and surrounded by a crowd of mourners. When Lincoln asked one of the soldiers who had died, the soldier replied 'The President'. He was killed by an assassin.' The interesting thing is that Lincoln insisted that the body on display in the vision was not his own. So he himself did not view the dream as a part of his own demise.

Abraham Lincoln was apparently interested in the meaning of angel dreams and what they might say about future events both positive and negative. Proof of his curiosity lies in an 1863 letter to his wife, who at the time was in Philadelphia with their 10-year-old son Todd Lincoln. Lincoln wrote to ask that Mary 'Put Todd's pistol away' as he had an ugly dream about him. Moreover, members of Lincoln's cabinet recalled that on the morning of his assassination the President told them he had dreamed of sailing across an unknown body of water at great speed. He also apparently revealed that he had the same dream repeatedly on previous occasions, before 'nearly every great and important event of the war'. These stories prove the great interest he took in the predictive power of angels.

Lincoln did not believe in an after-life – he believed that the soul loses identity after death – but some accounts argue that Lincoln changed his mind about those beliefs.

Abraham Lincoln died in 1865 but many people say that his spirit has lingered on, and they do not mean figuratively. Numerous White House residents and people have reported sightings of the 16th President's ghost. Some claim to have seen Lincoln's ghost at Ford's Theatre, where he was assassinated by Booth, while others claim to have seen his presence at Fort Monroe in Virginia or his tomb in Springfield. The majority of Lincoln's ghost sightings seem to be at the White House, where the President spent the final momentous years of his life. The Sixteenth President's apparition reportedly has been seen at the White House by a long list of people, including British Prime Minister Winston Churchill, Queen Wilhelmina of Netherlands and President Regan's daughter Maureen.

In fact, Abraham Lincoln's may be the most well-travelled ghost in history. Certainly there is no doubt that few presidents have left the sort of mark on the White House that he did. His impact on the history of America has been immeasurable and in 1864, when he sought re-election, he did so with the idea that his plans were unfinished. When he was assassinated, his plans for reconciliation between the North and South were interrupted and his work was left incomplete. In fact, some would say that it remains incomplete even today. Perhaps this is why his spirit is so often reported at the White House and may explain why he is the nation's most famous ghost.

Although there are few reports of Lincoln's spectre haunting the White House in the late nineteenth century, there are nonetheless suggestions that his spirit was present. In the years following his death, staff members and residents often reported mysterious footsteps in the hallways. One of the earliest reliable reports from someone who actually saw Lincoln's apparition came from President Theodore Roosevelt, who took up residence in the house nearly forty years after Lincoln's death. "I see him in different rooms and in the halls," he admitted. In truth, it comes as no surprise that Roosevelt may have "attracted" the ethereal presence of Lincoln as he greatly admired the former leader and quoted his speeches and writings often.

During the terms of President Calvin Coolidge, his wife Grace actually encountered Lincoln. She stated that he was dressed "in black, with a stole draped over his shoulders to ward off the drafts and chills of Washington's night air". She explained that one day as she passed by the Yellow Oval Room, she was startled to see Lincoln staring out the window in the direction of the Potomac, his hands behind his back. Lincoln turned and looked momentarily in her direction and then vanished. During his tenure in the White House, the room had been Lincoln's library and he often stood at the same window, looking out with his thoughts filled with the course of the war. At that same window,

Lincoln's spirit has also been seen and felt by others, including the poet and Lincoln biographer, Carl Sandburg. He also stated that he felt Lincoln's presence close to him in the Yellow Oval Room.

President Herbert Hoover also admitted to hearing mysterious sounds in the White House. Although he never acknowledged that it was Lincoln's ghost, Hoover left no doubt that he had heard something in the darkened corridors that he could not explain.

By the time Franklin Delano Roosevelt began his long series of terms as President, Lincoln had been dead for nearly seventy years. However, his ghost remained, unwilling or unable to leave the White House. During Roosevelt's administration, Lincoln was at his most active, perhaps because of concerns about the perilous state of the nation during the time of the Great Depression and World War II.

Eleanor Roosevelt told reporters that she had never seen Lincoln, but she admitted that she had felt his presence late at night when she used the Lincoln bedroom as a study. She often said that she sensed him, "standing behind her, peering over her shoulder". She also admitted that she sometimes heard his "footsteps in the second-floor hallways". Mrs. Roosevelt also told of an incident that occurred with one of her staff members, Mary Eben. Her secretary had passed the Lincoln bedroom one day and noticed a tall, thin man who was sitting on the edge of the bed, pulling on a pair of boots. She then realized that the figure was Abraham Lincoln. As the late president had been dead for about seventy-five years at the time, she was understandably frightened and ran screaming back to her office. Mary became just one of the many people who saw Lincoln's ghost during Roosevelt's time in the White House, including the President's valet, who once ran out of the mansion, shrieking in fear that he had just seen Abraham Lincoln.

In addition to the residents and staff members of the White House, a number of notable visitors also encountered Lincoln during this time. One story relates to Queen Wilhelmina of the Netherlands, who spent the night in the White House during the War years while in exile from the Nazis. It was said that she was sleeping in the Rose Room when she heard an insistent tapping on the door. As the hour was quite late, she assumed the summons must be important and she quickly opened the door. There, standing in the doorway, was Abraham Lincoln.

According to a White House staff member, the Queen surprised President Franklin D. Roosevelt and a number of cocktail party guests the next evening when she recalled her encounter. She told them that after seeing the apparition, everything went black and she later woke up on the floor. By this time, the ghost had vanished.

The late British Prime Minister Winston Churchill rarely discussed Lincoln's ghost, but many believe that he may have encountered him while visiting the White House. Churchill was always quartered in the Lincoln Bedroom during his stays, as were all visiting male heads of state, but the next morning, he would normally be found sleeping in a room across the hall. He confessed that he never felt comfortable in that particular room but mostly refused to discuss what made him so fearful of it.

Of all of the presidents who encountered Lincoln's ghost, the best known was President Harry S. Truman, who made no bones about the fact that he believed the White House to be haunted. He once recalled an incident that took place in the early morning hours, about one year after he took office. He was awakened that night by knocking on his bedroom door. He got out of bed, went to the door and opened it, but found that no one was in the hallway. Suddenly, the air around him felt icy cold but the chill quickly faded as President Truman heard the sound of footsteps moving away from him down the corridor.

He later wrote to his wife, Bess, who had stayed behind at their family home in Missouri because she didn't like Washington, and stated that, "I sit in this old house, all the while listening to the ghosts walk up and down the hallway. At four o'clock, I was awakened by three distinct knocks on my bedroom door. No one was there. Damned place is haunted, sure as shootin'!"

During his time in office, President Dwight D. Eisenhower made no effort to deny the experiences that he'd had with Lincoln's ghost. He told his press secretary, James Haggerty, that he frequently sensed Lincoln's ghost in the White House. One day, he explained that he was walking down a hallway and the ghost of Abraham Lincoln approached him from the opposite direction. Eisenhower took the encounter in stride – after the horrors of war, the spectre of Lincoln was probably a tame enough sight. Surprisingly, Haggerty told of the President's ghostly experience on a network television program, despite the long-held White House position on a strict "no ghost" policy.

Jacqueline Kennedy, who occupied the White House with her family and husband, John F. Kennedy, exactly one hundred years after the Lincolns lived there, admitted that she sensed Lincoln's presence in the mansion. Although there is no record of President Kennedy ever encountering the ghost, Jackie told reporters in 1961 that she found the White House to be "cold and drab" and disliked much of the furnishings. With this in mind, she undertook a major renovation. When she had completed the widely publicized refurbishment, the White House was freshly painted and redecorated. This is when Lincoln's ghost began to stir again. Possibly unsettled by the massive alterations in the house. It was during the restoration that Jackie began to encounter his ghost. When he occupied the White House, Lincoln had paid little attention to the furnishings and once was very angry with Mary when she spent too much money decorating "this damned old house".

Despite official denials, members of the first families continued to encounter Lincoln's spectre. When Gerald Ford was in office, his daughter, Susan, publicly acknowledged her belief in ghosts and made it clear that she would never sleep in the Lincoln Bedroom – or "that room", as she called it. According to one account, Susan actually witnessed Lincoln's spirit.

The late President Ronald Reagan even mentioned Lincoln's ghost in a 1987 press conference. He told the reporters who were gathered that he was never frightened by the spirit. "I haven't seen him myself," Reagan said, "but every once in a while, our little dog Rex will start down that long hall, just glaring as though he's seeing something." He also added that the dog would bark repeatedly as he stopped in front of the Lincoln bedroom. Reagan said that if he opened the door to the bedroom and tried to get the dog to come inside, Rex would growl fiercely but refused to step over the threshold.

As late as the 1980s, Maureen Reagan reported that she and her husband had seen Lincoln's ghost while staying in the Lincoln Bedroom. When she told her father about the apparition, he asked her to send Lincoln down the hall to his office the next time she saw him: 'I've got a few questions to ask him,' he said.

There were no reports of Lincoln's ghost during the Bush administration and both the President and Mrs. Bush denied seeing Lincoln or any other ghost in the White House. However, during the Clinton years, there were at least two sightings of Lincoln's apparition. One encounter was admitted by President Clinton's brother, Roger, who stated that he had sensed Lincoln's presence in the White House. In the second instance, a Clinton aide admitted that he had seen Lincoln walking down a hallway but the story, which was briefly reported in the news, was quickly denied and dismissed by the White House as a joke.

If the ghost of Abraham Lincoln does really still walk in the White House, the question is, why? Is the apparition merely a faded memory of another time or an actual presence? Does the ghost appear, as has been suggested, during times of crisis, when perhaps the assistance of the president who faced America's greatest crisis is most needed?

President Harry Truman had no idea why Lincoln's ghost was still present in the White House. In her biography about the president, Margaret Truman stated that her father certainly had no ambitions to haunt the White House himself. "No man in his right mind would want to come here of his own accord," he said.

It was British Prime Minister Winston Churchill's habit of an evening to take a long hot bath, and a stay at the White House was no cause for exception. After a hard day's work hashing out details of the war with Roosevelt, a bath, a good cigar, and a fine brandy were just what the doctor ordered. One evening, he soaked, sipped, and puffed for a good long while. Finally, satisfied with the results of his ritual ablutions, he emerged, dripping, and headed into the Lincoln Bedroom, where his hosts had chosen to accommodate him. There, leaning against the mantel, was the unmistakable figure of Abraham Lincoln.

Churchill stood stunned, cigar in one hand, half-empty glass in the other, naked as the day he was born. Thankfully, Churchill was rarely tongue-tied for long. 'Good evening, Mr. President,' he said. 'It seems you have me at a disadvantage. Lincoln's ghost apparently looked at him, smiled, and slowly faded away!

It's an amusing story. But one that may have deeper significance. Wouldn't it be nice to believe that in the midst of World War II, as Franklin Roosevelt and Winston Churchill met to coordinate the Allied assault against the Axis powers, the spirit of Abraham Lincoln was in the White House, guiding their endeavours?

There are dozens of similar stories about Lincoln's ghost haunting the executive mansion. One book of presidential ghost stories insists that 'so many sightings of Lincoln's ghost have been reported that it is, without question, the most frequently seen apparition in White House history'. Maids, butlers, guests, and staffers have said that they have seen Lincoln's spirit doing everything from pacing back and forth along a hallway, to pulling on his boots.

Whether or not ghosts exist, and whether Abraham Lincoln is one of them, remains a question better left to theologians. But it is undeniable that since his death in 1865, the notion that Lincoln's ghost is still present in the United States has resurfaced again and again in American popular culture.

Ordinary Americans from all walks of life have been drawn to the places that Lincoln lived and objects that he owned, in the belief that they serve as a conduit to his spirit. These examples demonstrate how memory functions not only as a set of ideas about the past but also as a living force in the present.

George Moses Horton, a poet and former slave living in Chatham County North Carolina, averred that an assassin's bullet could never truly kill Lincoln:

> Still weep, my soul, remain to weep;
> That one so noble thus should die;
> His spirit mount into the sky,
>
> His hallowed bones can only sleep.
> Still, still, the praise to him we give,
> Brave Presidents forever live!
>
> Whomever born must live to die –
> The King, the Regent and the Peer,
> And leave regardless of a tear,
> Down trickling from the weeping eye!
> The tears of sorrow may be shed,
> But Lincoln will never be dead!
> *George Moses Horton*

The American populace linked the spirit of Washington and Lincoln in the national consciousness, and imagining their reunion in heaven had deep emotional resonance for a country eager to see its much-loved former president rewarded for his sacrifice. 'If Lincoln possessed not his forerunner's unmatched and almost superhuman grandeur, he was more gentle and sweet' pronounced Reverend C. A. Bartol in a sermon reproduced in *The Monthly Religious Magazine* in July 1865, 'He was not Washington's facsimile, but counterpart. Heaven be blest for them both!'

Lincoln's assassination on Good Friday and his unintentional martyrdom quickly led to his assumption in the popular mind of a status akin to that of Jesus Christ. The parallel prompted writers and artists to cast Washington and Lincoln in the Biblical roles of Creator and Redeemer of the Nation, respectively.

The best way to understand the White House may be as a haunted house. By way of its paranormal history, its intense psychological pressures, and as a home that its residents are barred by tradition from leaving, the official residence belongs to the horror genre far more comfortably than inspiring emblem.

The facts of history make it clear that the place is lousy with ghouls. Multiple First Family members have noted strange and unexplained goings-on in their temporary abode. Truman wrote of hearing banging and scratches at his office door as he authorised the final development and deployment of the atom bomb. President Taft forbade mention of the spectre of a terrifying small boy who ran around the halls and was referred to as The Thing. Mary (and possibly also Abe) Lincoln conducted seances in its rooms. Reagan based a number of his most significant decisions on the counsel of a spiritualist.

Looking back through the presidential photo albums, few if any First Families have ever appeared truly at home in the mansion. Who could blame them? It's a structure surrounded by cameras yet deeply private; part office, part prison. But it's not just the discomfort of living in a whitewashed fishbowl that makes 1600 Pennsylvania Avenue a place of fear. The portraits on the walls (with whom Nixon carried on drunken conversations), the antique fireplaces (coming from which Jenna Bush repeatedly heard strange voices and piano music) – every feature of the place is stained by the past. And if, as observers of the paranormal point out, the most haunted places are where traumatic events (or consequential decisions) have occurred, the stains of the White House must be especially bloody.

"There's a lot of institutional history just within the architecture itself," says Lattanzi Shutika of George Mason University. "A lot of people believe that we leave imprints on the places we inhabit. We take a space, do our daily lives or interactions, we make them meaningful places. And the White House is, you know, when you think about the Republic, is one of the most meaningful places because it's the residency of the presidency".

The White House hosts its own ghostly gala of the illustrious dead.

Abraham Lincoln: Abraham Lincoln appears in the Lincoln Bedroom and Yellow Oval Room. First Lady Grace Coolidge, Prime Minister Winston Churchill, and Queen Wilhelmina of the Netherlands claim to have seen Lincoln.

Willie Lincoln: President Lincoln isn't the only one in his family haunting the White House. Lincoln's son Willie who died in the White House at the age of 11, most likely from typhoid fever, was reportedly seen not only by his parents but also by staff of the Grant administration in the 1870s.

Andrew Jackson: Andrew Jackson, Seventh President, is supposed to let out a guttural laugh while lying in his bed in the Queen's Bedroom (Rose

Room). The laugh has been heard in the White House since the 1860s. Mary Todd Lincoln claimed to have heard Jackson stomping and swearing.

Thomas Jefferson: In the 1860s President Jefferson was heard playing his violin in the Yellow Oval Room, prompting President Lincoln's wife Mary Todd to once marvel at a friend "My, my, how Mr. Jefferson does play that violin".

Dolley Madison: Dolley Madison, wife of James Madison, Fourth President protects the Rose Garden.

John Tyler: John Tyler, Tenth President, haunts the Blue Room with Julia Gardner, his second wife. Following the death of President Tyler's first wife, he proposed to Ms. Gardiner at Washington's Birthday Ball.

William Henry Harrison: William Henry Harrison, ninth President, haunts the attic. He was the first president to die in the White House.

Abigail Adams: The wife of the nation's Second President, John Adams, was the first First Lady to live in the White House. She used the East Room to dry sheets. Since her death in 1818, numerous residents and staffers claim to have seen her walking around with her arms outstretched, as if carrying clean linens. Forever doing laundry – what a harsh fate!

Unnamed British Soldier: An unnamed British Soldier who perished during the War of 1812 roams the White House grounds holding a torch.

David Burnes: In 1791, David Burns sold the government most of the land on which the White House and indeed the entire city of Washington DC, now sits, Since then, his voice has been heard by a guard and a valet in the Oval Office, apparently saying, 'I'm Mr Buuuuurns'.

Jeremiah Jerry Smith worked at the White House during the Ulysses S. Grant administration, as a footman, butler, cook, doorman and official duster, from the late 1860s until his retirement approximately 35 years later. He claimed to have seen the ghost of Lincoln, Grant, McKinley and several first ladies during his time there.

In 2009 then first lady Michelle Obama told visiting school children that she and President Barack Obama sometimes heard strange noises in the hallway at night.

If those noises were caused by the presence of Abraham Lincoln, I can only imagine that he was really proud to have an African American family in the White House after all the sacrifices he made.

The Obamas are not the sole White House occupants to report strange spiritual happenings at 1600 Pennsylvania Avenue.

In 1911, President Taft's military aide, Major Archibald Butt, wrote a letter to his sister referencing the ghost of a teenage boy that a White House maid had encountered. The maid apparently felt a slight pressure on her shoulder, as if someone were leaning over her. When Major Butt began to investigate her account, President Taft told him that the first member of the White House staff to repeat the ghost story would be fired.

David Burnes, the original owner of part of the land on which the White House now stands, sold his land in 1792 to make room for the White House. Mr. Burns' ghost has been seen and heard looming inside the White House

The White House Grounds

In late August of 1814, the White House was burned by British troops. A British soldier who died during the war has been seen roaming around the White House grounds with a torch.

The North Portico

It is rumoured that long deceased ushers and doormen can be seen manning their posts at the North Portico to this day. However, the most storied visitor of the North Portico is the ghost of Anna Surratt, and legend says the banging is Anna's ghost, rattling the doors and gates pleading for her mother's life.

Anna's mother, Mary, was hanged in 1865 after her conviction as a conspirator in the murder of Abraham Lincoln, becoming the only woman ever executed by the US. government. Anna's weeping still sometimes swells throughout the White House entrance hall, even with the doors shut! And on July 7th each year, the anniversary of her mother's execution, Anna's ghost paces back and forth on the front steps, supposedly awaiting the arrival of President Johnson. (President Andrew Johnson became President after Lincoln's assassination, and it was to him that Anna turned her pleas for her mother's life). Anna visited the White House one last time on the morning of July 7th 1865, in a last-ditch effort to save her mother. Each year on the anniversary of this day, Anna is said to sit on the front steps. There have also been many sightings of Anna banging on the White House doors, pleading for her mother's release.

What The Presidents' Children Saw

Margaret Truman, daughter of thirty-third President Harry Truman, constantly heard floors popping, doors knocking, and drapes sliding back and forth. Her father described the mansion as being haunted.Margaret decided to get to the bottom of the bizarre rap-tap-tappings, and one night, on a dare, slept in the Lincoln bedroom, the room haunted most by eerie thumps and bumps. President Truman must have known of his daughter's ghostly quest, for the only 'ghost' to appear that particular night was a White House butler wearing a top hat, a prank played by a light-hearted father. But Margaret's 'ghosts' persisted, prank or no prank, eventually prompting her father to order renovations,

Margaret and her father were not alone when hearing spooky noises in the White House. Jenna Bush, daughter of President W. Bush, Forty-Third President, awoke to music, describing her experience thus: "I was asleep. There was a fireplace in my room, and all of a sudden I heard 1920s music coming out. I could feel it. I freaked out and ran into my sister's room." Jenna's sister, Barbara, believed the story to be malarkey, real rubbish! But when Jenna dared Barbara to sleep in her room the following night, both heard an ear-splitting opera blaring from the exact same fireplace. No warm, cosy sleep for either that night – at first light, regular White House workers spilled the beans to the shaken sisters, stating "They heard it all the time".

Susan Ford, daughter of Thirty-Eighth President Gerald Ford, ran smack-dab into the spectre of Abraham Lincoln alongside the fireplace in the Lincoln bedroom. Scared to return to the room, Susan never entered again until, on a dare, she and a friend decided to sleep in that bedroom on her father's last night as president. The girls hoped to see Lincoln putting on his boots, just as one of Franklin Roosevelt's clerks had once seen. The risk paid off, but in an unexpected way. Susan awoke to see her mother, Elizabeth, dressed in a sheet, reciting the Gettysburg Address. "We were like, yeah mom, we're a little too old for that", Susan joked,

Similar to Susan, Maureen Regan bumped into Lincoln's spirit. She woke one morning in the Lincoln bedroom to - in the words of her father President Ronald Regan – "a figure standing at the window looking out. She could see the trees right through it. Again, it turned and disappeared". Apparently, Regan's dog, a spaniel named Rex, also sensed Lincoln's ghost, barking frantically near the door to the bedroom, but never setting foot inside. Rex also barked at the ceiling for no apparent reason as the Reagans watched TV.

Lynda Johnson Robb, daughter to Thirty-Sixth President Lyndon Johnson, met and maybe even spoke to the spirit of a fellow child of the White House, Willie Lincoln, who died from a fever at the age of 12. Willie's ghost visited Lynda in the very room in which he passed on. Willie's spirit, like that of his father, seems to flit and fly all around the house, dropping in on several White House staff members over the years, including a maid during the presidency of Ulysses S. Grant.

Amy Carter, Thirty-Ninth President Jimmy Carter's daughter, decided to "call upon" Lincoln's ghost one Halloween. She and a friend dared to spend a night in the Lincoln bedroom, consulting a Ouija board before falling to sleep. As Amy's mother Rosalynn jokes "Of course they heard the ghost," for mother and Amy's nurse Mary Fitzpatrick, pulled a hair-raising hoax. They covered themselves with sheets and "burst into the room to the young girls' screams".

Presidents of Faith
Obama

When President Obama, Forty-Fourth President published his book 'A Promised Land,' he invoked biblical imagery: A Land Promised by God to his people. Obama includes the role of religious institutions, faith leaders and personal traditions throughout the 750-page book. Friends and strangers have told him they believe God engineered his road to the White House, but Obama himself says he did not view his political path as a call from God.

'I suspect that God's plan whatever it is, works on a scale too large to admit our mortal tribulations; that in a single lifetime accidents and happenstance determine more than we care to admit', he writes, adding 'the best we can do is to try to align ourselves with what we feel is right and construct some meaning out of our confusion, and with grace and nerve play at each moment the hand that we're dealt.'

Obama tried to keep his prayer life private, and often mentions his 'broader scepticism toward organized religion' but says he often turned to private prayer. Not long after he was shown the Lincoln Bible on which he would be sworn in, Obama paused before entering the inaugural platform. 'For a brief moment, before trumpets sounded and I was announced I closed my eyes' he writes, 'and summoned the prayer that had carried me here, one I would continue to repeat every night I was President. A prayer of thanks for all I had been given. A prayer that my sins be forgiven. A prayer that my family and the American people be kept safe from harm. A prayer for guidance.'

Months before that moment, Obama had paid a visit to Jerusalem's western wall where pilgrims have long left petitions to God. He was at that stage feeling the weight of what lay ahead if he became President.

Obama was not superstitious, but he carried religious symbols among his collection of charms over the course of the campaign. He found himself making some concessions to the spirit world. He developed a habit of carrying five or so tiny momentums people had given him, including a lucky medal, a poker chip and a nun's silver cross. His assortment of charms grew steadily – a miniature buddha, an Ohio buckeye, a laminated four-leaf clover, a tiny bronze figure of Hanuman the Hindu monkey god, all manner of angels, rosary beads, crystals and rocks. He later called these 'a tactile reminder' of the people he had met and of their hopes. He figured that even if his cache of small treasures did not guarantee the universe would tilt in his favour, 'they didn't hurt' either.

Joshua Du Bois was spiritual advisor to Barack Obama and once said 'President Obama is a deeply faithful President and did not need a whole bunch of help cultivating that faith.' Barack Obama began his mornings with a devotion that DuBois sent him every day – Obama described these as 'snippets of scripture for me to reflect on by Blackberry.' He worshipped at churches as often as he got a chance. And occasionally,

DuBois revealed, the President would of his own volition request suggested Bible readings, for his personal use or as he was reflecting on important issues of the nation.

Instead of going to church every Sunday, Obama would occasionally summon pastors to him. These private Oval Office prayer sessions with some pastors dialling in by phone were rarely listed on his public schedule.

The biggest test of Obama's personal faith came late in his first term, when a gunman massacred twenty children and six adults at Sunday Hook Elementary School in Newton, Connecticut. Obama described the shooting and its aftermath as the worst days of his presidency. It also proved spiritually challenging, DuBois said, including an emotionally wrenching visit to Newtown to meet privately with grieving families of the community.

Obama mediated on 2 Corinthians 4:16-51:1 during and after Newtown to draw strength as a comforter. DuBois said the Bible passage reads in part: "Do not lose heart, though outwardly we are washing away inwardly we are being renewed day by day".

Obama has said he believes deeply that part of the bedrock strength of America is that it embraces people of many faiths and of no faith. Though it is a predominantly Christian country, Jews, Muslims, Hindus, Atheists, Agnostics, Buddhist all have their own path to grace, one that is revered and respected. That, Obama believes, is the part of what makes America what it is. Obama used his religion to make decisions; and nearly half (48 percent) of Americans in a poll stated that he relied on his religion the right amount when making policy choices.

Trump

In 2017 Melania Trump made headlines when she opened a campaign rally in Florida for husband Donald with The Lord's Prayer and a promise to raise awareness for women and children's issues across the World.

Melania is a practicing Roman Catholic. On her wedding day she was wearing her mother's rosary and later when she visited the Vatican and met Pope Francis, the First Lady asked him to bless the rosary, which he did. She placed flowers at the feet of a statue of The Virgin Mary and spent time praying at the Bambino Gesù Hospital during her visit. Melania was the first Catholic to live at 1600 Pennsylvania Avenue since President John F. Kennedy and his wife Jackie in the early 1960s. She married Donald Trump, a lifelong Presbyterian, in 2005 at an Episcopal Church in Palm Beach, Florida.

Donald Trump was obsessed with Abraham Lincoln and tried to measure himself to Lincoln's greatness. Trump has spoken at the Lincoln Memorial three times. Donald Trump's spiritual adviser and church leader Pastor Paula White said in an interview that her relationship with the President is the result of a direct 'assignment' from God, who directed her to 'show him who I am'. She is also described as the woman who 'led Trump to Christ'.

Biden

President Joe Biden says his belief is rooted in his cultural Catholicism. He is said to carry rosary beads in his pocket that belonged to his dead son, Beau. Even on election day he went to mass as he does every Sunday. In his victory speech he quoted from Ecclesiastes, "*The Bible tells us that to everything there is a season - a time to build, a time to reap, a time to sow and a time to heal. This is the time to heal in America*"

For only the second time in US History a Catholic will occupy the White House as the Forty-Sixth President. A man of profound faith, he has pledged to restore the 'Soul of the Nation' after four years of rancour.

He chose Kamala Harris as the Vice President who, as well as being the first woman of colour to hold the position, comes from a family that has embraced the Baptist church, Hinduism and Judaism.

Biden's Catholicism is at the core of his life and is likely to shape the way he governs as President. In his book 'Promises to Keep' on life and politics he wrote *"My idea of self, of family, of community, of the wider world comes straight from my religion. It's not so much the Bible, the beatitudes, the Ten Commandments, The Sacraments or the prayers I learned. It's the culture"* As President he added *"These are the principles that will shape all that I do, and my faith will continue to serve as my anchor, as it has my entire life"*.

One thing all the Presidents of the White House have in common was, regardless of their religious beliefs which have been the subject of much debates, the links between religion and mortality and the habits which lead to political prosperity, religion and mortality and in-dispensable support. Regardless of each president's beliefs' they all tried to craft the new nation, struggling with the question of how to impart morality and virtue to a diverse people. They could not achieve becoming President without divine power behind them. Powers or forces that are universal transcend human capacities. Without divine power in the ability or capacity to do things, personal, governmental, political or earthly power is limited; however divine power is unlimited and can do all things even the impossible.

When men want to construct a building, they look for a stable ground, establish foundations on it and then build. When God wants to build something great, he looks for unstable grounds and builds something on it. For example, men do not build on floods. But when God wanted to create the earth, the Bible says in Psalms 24:1-2:

"The earth is the Lord's and the fullness thereof; the world, and they that dwell therein. For he has founded it on the seas, and established it on the floods. Only God can do this."

Chapter 8

Angel Songs

In 2011, Robbie Williams said he wrote 'Angels', about his aunt and uncle, with collaborator Guy Chambers in 25 minutes. By his account, he and Chambers were sitting outside a cafe watching a water fountain, and this inspired them to write the chorus. In 2016, Williams said: "It was the first of our songs that we wrote together. We could tell and hoped and prayed that we got something incredibly special." Williams expressed irritation that some assumed Chambers was the sole author.

Irish singer-songwriter Ray Heffernan asserts that in fact he wrote the first version of 'Angels,' in Paris in 1996, after his partner had a miscarriage. According to Heffernan, he met Williams by chance in a pub in Dublin. He showed him an incomplete version of the song, and that week the two recorded a studio demo. Williams confirmed that he had recorded a demo with Heffernan but said he rewrote the song significantly with Chambers.

Before the song's release, Heffernan accepted an offer from Williams's management to buy the rights for £7,500. He is thanked in the UK CD single liner notes. Williams said: "We could have gone to court, and it all would have been down to whether the judge wakes up that day out of bed... So I gave him some money, and he went away." In 2011, Heffernan said: "For a long time, I was angry about this, but as you get older you see things differently ... The 'Angels' connection has opened doors to publishing companies and earned me a few quid."

Angels – Robbie Williams

I sit and wait
Does an angel contemplate my fate?
And do they know the places where we go
When we're grey and old?
'Cause I've been told
That salvation lets their wings unfold
So when I'm lying in my bed
Thoughts running through my head
And I feel that love is dead
I'm loving angels instead

[Chorus]
And through it all
She offers me protection
A lot of love and affection
Whether I'm right or wrong
And down the waterfall
Wherever it may take me
I know that life won't break me
When I come to call
She won't forsake me
I'm loving angels instead

When I'm feeling weak
And my pain walks down a one-way street

I look above
And I know I'll always be blessed with love
And as the feeling grows
She breathes flesh to my bones
And when love is dead
I'm loving angels instead

[Chorus]
And through it all
She offers me protection
A lot of love and affection
Whether I'm right or wrong
And down the waterfall
Wherever it may take me
I know that life won't break me
When I come to call
She won't forsake me
I'm loving angels instead
[Instrumental Bridge]

[Chorus]
And through it all
She offers me protection
A lot of love and affection
Whether I'm right or wrong
And down the waterfall
Wherever it may take me
I know that life won't break me
When I come to call
She won't forsake me
I'm loving angels instead

What are the lyrics to "Hark! The Herald Angels Sing" – and what's the story behind the carol?

The lyrics for 'Hark! The Herald Angels Sing' were written by Methodist Charles Wesley in 1739, and they first appeared in the collection *Hymns and Sacred Poems*. But Charles Wesley's words were sung to a somewhat gloomy melody.

Today, in the best-known version, we sing Wesley's words adapted by the English musician William H. Cummings to fit the joyous tune written by Felix Mendelssohn, originally known as 'Vaterland, In Deinen Gauen'.

This is one of the most widely sung carols, a favourite among buskers and choristers. And yet, you may well be unaware of the fascinating story behind it.

Today, the version of 'Hark! The Herald Angels Sing' that we're familiar with generally stays true to the fine details of Cummings' adaptation (particularly its harmonisation).

But over the years, composers have written descants for the final verse. Perhaps the most famous is the one written by Sir David Willcocks in 1961 for the annual *Festival of Nine Lessons and Carols* at King's College, Cambridge

What is 'Hark! The Herald Angels Sing' actually about?

Well, the purpose of the carol was to explore the spiritual theme of eco-theology, linking Christ's intention to redeem not only humankind, but nature as a whole.

Hear it in the words '*Peace on earth and mercy mild, God and sinners reconciled*' in verse one, and '*Light and life to all He brings, Risen with healing in His wings*' in verse three.

Hark! The Herald Angels Sing

Hark! The herald angels sing,
"Glory to the newborn King!
Peace on earth and mercy mild,
God and sinners reconciled."
Joyful, all ye nations rise,
Join the triumph of the skies,
With the angelic host proclaim:
"Christ was born in Bethlehem."
Hark! The herald angels sing,
"Glory to the newborn King!"

Christ by highest heav'n adored,
Christ the everlasting Lord!
Late in time behold Him come,
Offspring of a Virgin's womb.
Veiled in flesh the Godhead see,
Hail the incarnate Deity,
Pleased as man with man to dwell,
Jesus, our Emmanuel.
Hark! The herald angels sing,
"Glory to the newborn King!"

Hail the heav'n-born Prince of Peace!
Hail the Son of Righteousness!
Light and life to all He brings,
Risen with healing in His wings.
Mild He lays His glory by,
Born that man no more may die,
Born to raise the sons of earth,

Born to give them a second birth.
Hark! The herald angels sing,
"Glory to the newborn King!"

The beloved Christmas hymn, "O Come, All Ye Faithful," is also a song about arrival. But now, the invitation is not for the Lord, as in Advent, but for God's faithful people.

When the angels had left them and gone into heaven, the shepherds said to one another, "Let's go to Bethlehem and see this thing that has happened, which the Lord has told us about."

"O Come, All Ye Faithful," Latin original by John Francis Wade (c. 1743), English translation by Frederick Oakeley, 1852.

O Come All Ye Faithful

O come, all ye faithful,
Joyful and triumphant!
O come ye, O come ye to Bethlehem;
Come and behold him
Born the King of Angels:

O come, let us adore Him,
O come, let us adore Him,
O come, let us adore Him,
Christ the Lord.

Sing, choirs of angels,
Sing in exultation,
Sing, all ye citizens of Heaven above!
Glory to God
In the highest:

Yea, Lord, we greet thee,
Born this happy morning;
Jesus, to thee be glory given!
Word of the Father,
Now in flesh appearing!

O come, let us adore Him,
O come, let us adore Him,
O come, let us adore Him,
Christ the Lord.
Amen.

Leonard Cohen's 'Anthem': That's how the light gets in

Leonard Cohen once explained the meaning of the song as follows:

"That is the background of the whole record, I mean if you have to come up with a philosophical ground, that is "Ring the bells that still can ring." It's no excuse… the dismal situation and the future is no excuse for an abdication of your own personal responsibilities towards yourself and your job and your love. 'Ring the bells that still can ring': they're few and far between but you can find them. 'Forget your perfect offering', that is the hang-up, that you're gonna work this thing out. Because we confuse this idea and we've forgotten the central myth of our culture which is the expulsion from the garden of Eden. This situation does not admit of solution or perfection. This is not the place where you make things perfect, neither in your marriage, nor in your work, nor anything, nor your love of God, nor your love of family or country. The thing is imperfect. And worse, there is a crack in everything that you can put together, physical objects, mental objects, constructions of any kind. But that's where the light gets in, and that's

where the resurrection is and that's where the return, that's where the
repentance is. It is with confrontation, with the brokenness of things."
— from Diamonds in the Line

That's How The Light Gets In

The birds they sang
At the break of day
Start again
I heard them say
Don't dwell on what has passed away
Or what is yet to be

Ah, the wars they will be fought again
The holy dove, she will be caught again
Bought and sold, and bought again
The dove is never free

Ring the bells that still can ring
Forget your perfect offering
There is a crack, a crack in everything
That's how the light gets in

We asked for signs
The signs were sent
The birth betrayed
The marriage spent
Yeah, and the widowhood
Of every government
Signs for all to see

I can't run no more
With that lawless crowd
While the killers in high places
Say their prayers out loud
But they've summoned, they've summoned up
A thundercloud
They're going to hear from me

Ring the bells that still can ring
Forget your perfect offering
There is a crack, a crack in everything
That's how the light gets in

You can add up the parts
But you won't have the sum
You can strike up the march
There is no drum
Every heart, every heart
To love will come
But like a refugee

Ring the bells that still can ring
Forget your perfect offering
There is a crack, a crack in everything
That's how the light gets in
Ring the bells that still can ring
Forget your perfect offering
There is a crack, a crack in everything
That's how the light gets in

Chapter 9

Angel of Calcutta & Angel of Hearts

Mother Teresa inspired Princess Diana to turn to charity work. Letters written by Diana reveal how a trip to Calcutta in India changed her life forever. She and Mother Teresa met when Diana visited the convent at a time when her marriage to Charles began to fall apart. Diana was inspired to help the poor by what she saw there.

Diana was very, very spiritual. Her experience of praying with the Sisters of Charity and seeing sick and dying children set her on a new path.

"I'd like to be a queen in people's hearts" Princess Diana

Diana felt that Mother Teresa caused a spiritual awakening on that first visit, which was followed by a visit to Mother Teresa's home. Diana was given a string of rosary beads during her visit.

'*I was then taken by Sister Federica to the chapel to pray with the novices and sisters*'.

They sang the Lord's Prayers and with our shoes off we prayed together on our knees'

Mother Teresa brought meaning to Diana's life. After meeting with sick children in February 1992, the Princess of Wales returned home and wrote a prayer and sent it to her butler Paul Burrell.

An accompanying note spoke of a profound awakening after praying with the nuns. 'Today, something very profound touched my life. I went to Mother Teresa's home and found the direction I've been searching for all these years,' the princess wrote.

'The sisters sang to me, a deeply spiritual experience and I soared to such heights in my spirit. The light shone from within these ladies, saints for want of a better word, such love came from their eyes and their touch was full of warmth.'

She now had a mission and she found a deep spirituality with Mother Teresa. They were so close. There's no doubt that this was the inspiration for all of the princess's wonderful humanitarian work.

"The greatest problem in the world today is intolerance.
Everyone is so intolerant of each other."
Princess Diana

During the visit to India where Diana was famously photographed sitting alone at the Taj Mahal 10 months after she divorced Charles, she experienced profound change. She later said that time had changed her life forever, and that she believed that the nuns were angels sent to Earth to do God's work.

"Anywhere I see suffering, that is where I want to be, doing what I can," Diana once said. She believed she wasn't worthy to even walk in Mother Teresa's footsteps, but that she could at least try to follow her example. Mother Teresa died five days after Diana's death, so close that some have speculated that they went to Heaven together.

"I think the biggest disease the world suffers from in this day and age
is the disease of people feeling unloved. I know that I can give love for
a minute, for half an hour, for a day, for a month, but I can give.
I am very happy to do that, I want to do that." Princess Diana

When Princess Diana died in that faithful car crash on August 3 1997, her body was taken from the operating theatre, and a vigil was kept over it by a Catholic priest, Father Yves-Marie Clochard-Bossuet, the duty chaplain who had been summoned from his bed to attend to Princess Diana. Madame Chirac, the President's wife, arrived around 9am and she stayed and prayed in the room where Diana's body lay along with Fr. Yves who, at the request of Madame Chirac, watched over her body for ten hours. An Anglican clergyman by the name of Martin Draper who was the serving Anglican Archdeacon of France arrived and prayed the Anglican prayer for the dead. A picture of Diana's two sons, which was in her handbag, had been placed in her hands, together with the rosary beads given to her by Mother Teresa.

"Carry out a random act of kindness, with no expectation of reward,
safe in the knowledge that one day someone might do the same for you."
Princess Diana

But who was Mother Teresa?

Mother Teresa was also known as St. Teresa of Calcutta. She was indeed an angel. She was born to Albanian parents in Skopje, present day Macedonia, named Anjeze, and lived a very calm and comfortable life. But all that changed when her father died suddenly.

Anjeze learned about Catholicism in school, and felt the calling and pull of missionary work abroad. At the age of 18, she joined the Loreto Sisters of Dublin in Ireland. A year later, she was sent to the Loreto Novitiate in Darjeeling, India – a move that would change her life forever. It was there that she adopted the name Teresa, after St Thérèse of Lisieux.

"I am not sure exactly what heaven will be like, but I know that when we die and it comes time for God to judge us, he will not ask, 'How many good things have you done in your life?' rather he will ask, "How much love did you put into what you did?" Mother Teresa

While in India, Teresa took a job teaching history and geography at a private wealthy school in Calcutta. But she began to feel bothered by the way the wealthy, well-to-do students lived, and the practical realities of slum life around the city. When she was 36 years old, the woman who would become known to the world as Mother Teresa had an epiphany. On 10 September 1946, Teresa experienced what she later described as "the call within the call", while travelling by train to the Loreto convent in Darjeeling from Calcutta for her annual retreat.

"I was to leave the convent and help the poor while living among them. It was an order. To fail would have been to break the faith." One author later observed, "Though no one knew it at the time, Sister Teresa had just become Mother Teresa".

Teresa realised that she could make a greater impact by venturing out of the convent and fostering an intimate and meaningful connection to India's poor among the slums.

After receiving her call, Teresa got permission to leave the convent and became a missionary. She took a crash course in nursing and later headed back to Calcutta where she opened a school for the poor. The simple power of Teresa's ministry spread quickly. As the resources grew, the scope of Teresa's work expanded as well.

"Not all of us can do great things. But we can do small things with great love." Mother Teresa

Mother Teresa set out her path, because she wanted to address the specific problems that came from over-crowding and limited resources. Mother Teresa's vision was to help and live among the poorest of the poor in the slums. Her efforts quickly caught the attention of Indian officials, including the Prime Minister who expressed his appreciation. Mother Teresa wrote in her diary that her first year was fraught with difficulties. She had no income and often had to resort to begging for food and supplies.

Mother Teresa experienced doubt, loneliness and the temptation to return to the comfort of the Convent life during these early months. At one point she wrote in her diary –

> *"Our Lord wants me to be a free nun covered with the poverty of the cross.*
>
> *Today I learned a good lesson, the poverty of the poor must be so hard for them. While looking for a home I walked and walked until my arm and legs ached. I thought about how much they must ache in body and soul, looking for a home, food and health. Then, the comfort of Loreto—"* (her former congregation) – *"came to tempt me; you have only to say the word and all that will be yours again, the tempter kept on saying.' But Theresa resisted. "Of free choice, my God and out of love for you, I desire to remain and do whatever be your holy will in my regard. I did not let a single tear come."*

For years, Mother Teresa refused to talk about the moment she decided to devote herself to the service of the poor. But she once said *"God called me to surrender to myself and to his service"*. Mother Teresa often bemoaned the 'darkness, loneliness and torture' she was undergoing. She compared the experience to hell and said it drove her to doubt the existence of God.

"If you are humble nothing will touch you, neither praise nor disgrace, because you know what you are." Mother Teresa

She never saw her family after she came to India. Her mother and sister are buried in Albania. She was always keen on taking part in the activities of her organisation. But in the 80's her health started to deteriorate and she even attempted to resign from her mission. Her secret letters show that she spent almost 50 years without sensing the presence of God in her life. What does her experience teach us about the value of doubt?

She began her missionary work with the poor in 1948, replacing her traditional Loreto habit with a simple white cotton sari decorated with a blue border. Mother Teresa adopted Indian citizenship, spent a few months in Panta to receive a basic medical training in the Holy Family Hospital and then ventured out into the slums.initially, she started a school in Motijhil (Calcutta); soon she started tending to the needs of the destitute and starving. In the beginning of 1949, she was joined in her effort by a group of young women and laid the foundations of a new religious community helping the "poorest among the poor".

Her efforts quickly caught the attention of Indian officials, including the prime minister, who expressed his appreciation. Teresa wrote in her diary that her first year was fraught with difficulties. She had no income and had to resort to begging for food and supplies.

On the 7th October 1950, Mother Teresa received Vatican permission to start the diocesan congregation that would become the Missionaries of Charity. Its mission was to care for, in her own words: *"The hungry, the naked, the homeless, the crippled, the blind, the lepers and all those people who feel unwanted, unloved, uncared for throughout society, people that have become a burden to society and are shunned by everyone."*

It began as a small congregation with 13 members in Calcutta. By 1997 it had grown to more than 4,000 sisters running orphanages, aids, hospices and charity centres worldwide; caring for refugees, the blind, disabled, aged, alcoholics, the poor and homeless, and victims of floods and epidemics and famine.

In 1952, Mother Teresa opened the first home for the dying in space made available by the city of Calcutta. With the help of Indian officials, Mother Teresa converted an abandoned Hindu temple into the Kalighat Home For The Dying, a free hospice for the poor. Mother Teresa renamed it Kalighat, The Home of the Pure Heart. Those brought to the home received medical attention and were afforded the opportunity to die with dignity.

"At the end of life we will not be judged by how many diplomas we have received, how much money we have made, how many great things we have done. We will be judged by "I was hungry, and you gave me something to eat, I was naked and you clothed me. I was homeless, and you took me in". Mother Teresa.

According to the rituals of their faith, Muslims were read the Quran, Hindus received water from the Ganges, and Catholics received the last rites; 'a beautiful death'. Mother Teresa said *"it's for people who lived like animals to die like angels – loved and wanted".*

Mother Teresa suffered a heart attack in Rome in 1983 while visiting Pope John Paul II. After a second attack in 1989, she received an artificial pacemaker. In 1991, after having pneumonia while in Mexico, she suffered further heart problems.

She offered to resign her position as head of the Missionaries of Charity, but the sisters of the congregation, in a secret ballot, voted for her to stay. Mother Teresa agreed to continue her work as head of the congregation.

In April 1996, Mother Teresa fell and broke her collarbone. In August she suffered from malaria and failure of the left heart ventricle. She had heart surgery but it was clear that her health was declining. The Archbishop of Calcutta, Henry Sebastian D'Souza, said he ordered a priest to perform an exorcism of Mother Teresa with her permission when she was first hospitalised with cardiac problems because he thought she may be under attack by the devil.

Christopher Hitchens accused her of hypocrisy for opting to receive advanced treatment for her heart condition.

On 13 March 1997, she stepped down from the head of Missionaries of Charity, She died 5 September 1997.

Her fame can be in large part attributed to the 1969 documentary Something Beautiful for God, which was filmed by Malcolm Muggeridge and his 1971 book of the same title. Muggeridge was undergoing a spiritual journey of his own at the time.

During the filming of the documentary, footage taken in poor lighting conditions, particularly the Home for the Dying, was thought unlikely to be of usable quality by the crew. After returning from India, however, the footage was found to be extremely well lit.

Muggeridge claimed this was a miracle of "divine light" from Mother Teresa herself. Others in the crew said it was due to a new type of ultra sensitive Kodak film. Muggeridge later converted to Catholicism. Around this time, the Catholic world began to honour Mother Teresa publicly.

In 1971, Paul VI awarded her first Pope John XXIII Peace Price, commending her for her work with the poor, display of Christian charity and efforts for peace. She later received the Pacem in Terris Award (1976). Since her death, Mother Teresa has progressed rapidly along the steps towards sainthood, currently having reached the stage of having been beatified.

By the time of her death, Angel Mother Teresa had devoted 69 years of service to the poor, and had set up 4,500 missionaries of charities working worldwide. She had 124 awards earned, including the Nobel Prize and the Bharat Ratna. In 2003, her beneficiation was attended by over 350,000 people; over 500,000 people attended her canonisation ceremony in Rome.

"Yesterday is gone, Tomorrow has yet to come. We have only today. Let us begin. I am the Lord God who lives in me and yet the reality of darkness and coldness and emptiness is so great that nothing touches my soul. Let us always meet each other with a smile for the smile is the beginning of love".

Mother Teresa

Chapter 10

Valley of Angels, Gyanganj, The Hill of Tara & Valley of Flowers

Angels live in the unseen heavenly realm. They have access to God, the Supreme, whose presence dwells above the heavens, and nature. Though angels have their residence in heaven, they are able to come to earth. They are spoken of as both ascending and descending. Therefore they are not restricted to any part of the universe. Consequently, they do the will of God whenever they are needed.

The mythic Valley of Angels is also known as Gyanganj, and believed to be located where the Mount Kailash mountain range is surrounded by many lakes, including Lake Manasarovar in China and Lake Rakshastal in Tibet. Mount Kailash is considered to be sacred in four religions: Hinduism, Bon, Buddhism and Jainism.

The name is derived from the word 'Kelāsa' which means "crystal". It is believed to be at the centre of the earth. Gyanganj is part of the magnificent and heavenly Himalayan Mountain Range that spans seven countries and has more than thirty-one peaks, and is believed to hide some of the deepest secrets. One such secret is this City of Immortal Beings.

Several attempts have been made over the years by mountaineers and trekkers to find the exact location of this divine city. So far, all their efforts have led to nothing – even the new age satellites and other mapping technologies have failed to map it.

There are several references to the Gyanganj in Hindu scriptures. It is mentioned in several texts. The old Tibetan Vedas (the most ancient and most important of all Hindu sacred literature) refer to it as 'Shyamala' or 'Sangrila.' Ancient Indian and Tibetan tales suggest that this place is a city of mysterious and immortal beings that cannot be discovered by ordinary men. Believers say that it is this celestial kingdom that influences the existence of humans in subtle ways whenever needed.

It is also said that the sacred city is so camouflaged that no mapping technique can ever identify the place. It is said that Gyanganj does not belong to any dimension, and that no religion or culture has any authority over it. It has its own independence and preserves the sacred and spiritual teachings of the world. In all probability Gyanganj has no permanent physical form but largely exists as a spiritual or energy field. On certain occasions Gyanganj manifests into physical beings for karmic reasons.

Shyamla is a Sanskrit word which means the source of happiness. The idea of a lost kingdom somewhere in the Himalayas has circulated in Buddhist Tibetan teaching for centuries. Some old Vedas texts include instructions to find Shyamla but the directions are obscure and only enlightened yogis would be able to locate it.

The name Shyamla first appeared in a text known as Kalachakra Tantra. The Kalachakra concept belongs to the highest level of Buddhist teaching. The tale describes a land behind the Himalayas that is only perceptible through yogic realisation. This land is also called Siddhashram, with a 4th dimensional form.

The stories say that the land of Shyamla lies in a valley, it is only approachable via a ring of snow peaks like the petals of a lotus. At the centre is a nine-story crystal mountain that stands over a sacred lake, and a palace adored with gold gems. Shyamla is a kingdom where humanity's wisdom is spared from the destruction and corruptions of time and history, ready to save the world in the hour of need.

The prophecy of Shyamla states that each of its 32 kings will rule for a hundred years. As their reign passes, conditions in the outside world will deteriorate; men will become obsessed with war and materialism will triumph over all spiritual life. Eventually an evil torrent will emerge to suppress the Earth in a reign of terror. But just when the world seems on the brink of a total downfall and destruction, the mists will lift to reveal the icy mountains of Shyamla. Then the 32nd King of Shyamla will lead a mighty army against the tyrants and in a great last battle, peace will be restored.

In his book *Autobiography Of A Yogi*, Paramhansa Yogananda wrote about his meeting with the great Guru Babaji. He described him as still alive in the Badrinath regions of the Himalayas, and that despite his great age he retained the appearance of a young man. The Guru was connected with Gyanganj, as was the Guru of Gopinath Kaviraj, who also wrote about those mysterious places.

Yogananda's own teacher, Swami Vishwa Pranab, had told him about the time he spent in Gyanganj, learning about solar science. The practice of that knowledge enabled him to manifest various objects and transform one thing into another by manipulating the sun rays.

Yogananda described a meeting with Guru Babaji in Calcutta where he witnessed his ability to manifest various perfumes on demand. Dr. Paul Brunton, in his search for secret India, also reported the same, and claimed he saw him revive a dead bird.

There are many accounts that draw a similar description of Gyanganj, a place that seems to be similar to Atlantis or somewhere out of King

Arthur's legend. Gyanganj is generally described as a Plateau in Tibet lying North of Kailash. There are many other locations scattered throughout India that are known as Gyanganj territory – including parts of the banks of the Alaknanda river and the Mandakini river beds. All the region from Rishikesh (the city known as the Gateway to the Garhwal Himalayas), to Mount Kailash, and from Yamunotri (the westernmost shrine in the Garhwal Himalayas), to Nanda Devi, India's second highest mountain. This has been part of the ancient texts since the time of immorality.

No one knows when the gates of Gyanganj will open again. It is truly a 4th dimensional place where many angels, like Babaji Maharaj, live. Only people who have a Kundalini awakening can experience Gyanganj, although this is a place every astral traveller wishes to visit. This un-invisible, untraceable sacred place is truly the Valley of Angels.

Three months ago I got a vision from my angels to visit the Hill of Tara. It was a divine vision. My angels requested me to go and visit this sacred site. The Hill of Tara is the jewel in the crown of the Boyne Valley landscape. From the top of the Hill of Tara, on a clear day you will see the panoramic views of Ireland's beautiful countryside from the flat plains of the Curragh in County Kildare, almost 5000 acres. Views of the Hill of Allen to the Boyne Valley. Some of the world's most mythical landscapes dating from the Neolithic period, including the megalithic passage graves of Knowth, Newgrange and Dowth. These passage tombs were constructed in around 3300 BC. They continued to be used for habitation and virtual purposes until the early Bronze Age, during which a number of embanked, pit and wooden posts circles (collectively referred to as "henges") were built.

Restored to its former glory, the Newgrange mound is a solid structure that's 250 feet across and 40 feet high, covering one acre of land. A tribute to its builders, the roof has remained essentially intact and waterproof for over 5,000 years. Both summer and winter Solstice are still celebrated today on this sacred site.In Pagan traditions, the legend of the Oak

King and the Holly King were told to explain the Summer and Winter Solstices.

On the 21st of June, the Oak King is reputedly at his strongest. Gradually his power weakens, until the Winter Solstice in the depths of Winter. This is when the Holly King regains power.

For northern hemisphere dwellers, Summer Solstice - the longest day and the shortest night of our year - is usually celebrated on June 21st.

In Gaelic, Solstice is "Grianstad", literally 'sun-stop' and this is one of the two great peak moments of the light and dark interplay in our universe. However, it is the earth which is on an elliptical orbit around the sun which uniquely brings about this phenomenon.

For several days after June 20th, the hours and minutes of daylight will remain almost exactly the same and near June 25th, the light will imperceptibly begin to lessen as we move deeper into the second half of this season. In terms of light, Summer Solstice day is 9 hours, 30 minutes longer than on Winter Solstice in December.

As a sunflower will twist and turn throughout the day to face the sun, when we humans look upwards, open to the solar energies of Summer Solstice, we are no longer separated from ourselves or the environment. Our ancestors saw this key turning point in the Celtic calendar as momentous – a time of blooming, blossoming and wild abandon. Even though it does herald the light starting to lessen, we can imagine they revelled in the height of summer and the fresh earthy freedom seeking new pleasures before Harvest.

The eternal ancestral voice from spiritual traditions is remembered in ceremonies and rituals in nature that can remind us who, where and what we really are. It is a traditional time for weddings, fires, garlands of colourful blossoms, and dance rituals.

For a species that defines being spiritualised as enlightenment, the peak moment of light on our planet is extremely special. We are consumers of light through our diet made possible by photosynthesis. Many healing modalities are built on the phenomenon of our body chakra system as being made of this.

No matter how we find our lives at this time, we cannot be immune from the abundance of light, heat, radiation and electromagnetic energy peaking in our natural world. That immensity is poetically evoked in one of the great mythological stories of Ireland.

Our ancestors had many references to deify the sun, the outstanding is Lugh the Sun God, known as Lugh Samhildánach or Lugh of the Many Arts. His entry to the court of King Nuada of the Tuatha Dé Danann (in Gaelic the "Tribe of Mother Earth") at Tara, the nexus of supreme power, was only possible by his response to the tests heaped upon him by the gatekeeper.

The Winter Solstice is an astronomical phenomenon marking the shortest day and the longest night of the year. It occurs when one of the earth's poles has its maximum slant away from the sun and it happens twice in each hemisphere at the peak of winter and summer. The solstices, the seasons and the changing length of daylight hours throughout the year are all due to one fact: the earth spins on a tilted axis.

The sun makes a sine wave across the sky over the course of the year, sometimes farther south or farther north. When the sun is 23.5 south in latitude and directly over the Tropic of Capricorn, which occurs on and around December 21st, the Winter Solstice takes place. At its farthest southern point, having moved slowly since last June, the sun "stops" for approximately three days before it starts to slowly creep back north again. During this time, there is a peak moment of the Solstice.

In our Celtic landscapes, the Winter Solstice is an ancient seasonal rite of passage that is ageless. We do know not when our ancestors first stood together and paused in harmony at midwinter. Our sacred sites such as the world famous Brú na Bóinne or NewGrange, aligned to the morning's rising sun, tell us that the Winter Solstice was important enough over 5,000 years ago to build a temple to this poignant solar event.

At dawn on the mornings surrounding the solstice, a narrow beam of light enters the 62 foot long passage and lights the floor. It moves along the ground, from the window box until it lights the rear chamber. The Neolithic light show lasts 17 minutes.Ancient carvings can be seen on many of the massive, kidney-shaped mound's curb stones, including the triple-spiral design synonymous with Newgrange.

In Irish, the Winter Solstice is "An Grianstad", literally translating as "the sun stop". This accuracy in describing the sun's intercourse with the earth helps us to momentarily stop also and integrate our fast moving modern lives with the plateau of maximum darkness and minimum light. These days of Winter Solstice time are precious, the pinnacle of a darkening that calls us to rest, be still, recover and dream. The minutes of sunlight in our days will eventually begin to increase towards that other great day of the season, Christmas Day.

The experience of darkness is such a different condition to light and is often sadly stigmatised. We are so accustomed to beginning things when the light is turned on, when the sun rises and when we open our eyes and adjust. Yet nature says the beginnings are in the dark. Life first is dreamed and vibrates in the absence of light. The seeds sown in autumn germinate underground through winter before appearing as shoots in spring. Each one of us reading this lived our first nine months or thereabouts in our mother's dark womb.

Our ancestors intuitively understood this phenomenon, acknowledging the new day at dusk and the New Year at Samhain (Halloween). They regarded the time between Samhain and the climax of the seasonal darkness of Winter Solstice as the treasured dreamtime of new life. Nature invites us to stir ourselves as courageous and passionate dreamers and to be in synchronicity with the great natural hibernation about us. Our invitation is to birth new prayers, new wishes, new intentions and new manifestations for ourselves and for our world.

Many still gather at Brú na Bóinne on Winter Solstice morning. While the chosen few who have won the lottery will be inside at sunrise at 8.36am, hundreds more will sing and dance or simply stand in awe. If skies are clear, the golden orb of the Sun peaks above Red Hill. If lucky, those in the Cairn may witness the sunlight snaking its way through the lightbox up the ancient path to penetrate the centre of this stunning architectural monument to a magnificent feat of nature. That this still occurs 5,000 years after Brú na Bóinne was built is itself an enthralling phenomenon.

The Summer and Winter Solstices were one of 8 Celtic festivals celebrated throughout the year.

0 Samhain: 1st November
1 Winter Solstice: 21st December
2 Imbolc: 2nd February
3 Spring Equinox: 21st March
4 Bealtaine: 1st May
5 Summer Solstice: 21st June
6 Lughnasadh: 1st August
7 Autumn Equinox: 21-24 September

"Fairies, come take me out of this dull world … And dance upon the mountains like a flame".

William Butler Yeats.

The Boyne River reflects like a mirror from the top of Tara, spanning 70 miles long, the Boyne River has been known since ancient times from the Battle of Boyne, a major battle in Irish History, took place along the Boyne near Drogheda in 1690 during the Williamite War in Ireland.

Fabulous views of Wicklow Mountains National Park covering 20,843 hectares with views of Glendalough's Monastic sites the ruins of the ancient site are scattered throughout the Valley can be seen from Tara. Many are almost 1000 years old. St. Kevin crossed these mountains from Hollywood to Glendalough in the latter part of the Sixth Century. Within a 100 years, the area had developed from a remote hermitage into one of the most important monastic sites in Ireland. The Monastery continued to flourish after St. Kevin's death in 617 AD.

Standing tall in the distance is the Round Tower of Monasterboice, one of Ireland's earliest Christian sites, the name derives from the Irish "Mainistir Bhuithe" (Monastery of Buite). St. Buite was an Irish Monk and follower of St. Patrick. It is said that in 480, St. Buite on a return trip from Rome raised Nechtan Morbet the King of Pictland (Scotland) from the dead. Today from Tara you can see the Round Tower, the magnificent High Crosses and the remains of two churches. Today the image of the high cross is recognised internationally, not merely as a religious icon but also as a symbol of Irish cultural heritage.

The Hill of Tara is one of the most iconic archaeological landscapes in Ireland. As the majority of Tara's buildings were constructed from timber the site appears today as a series of earth works and grassy banks and ditches. When you first visit the site it can be a little difficult to get a true sense of the phenomenal concentration of archaeology of Tara and the site certainly requires visitors to use their imagination. However at such an evocative and atmospheric place it is not very hard to conjure visions of ancient Temples, Palaces and Tombs.

At Tara only a thin veil exists between archaeology and mythology, history and legend. Irish antiquarian Robert R. Callery described Tara as the font of our Nationhood, the cradle of our faith, the seat of Kings and the home of Saints. It is truly a hallowed spot with such a vista it's no wonder that it became the ritual centre of Kingship and ceremony in Ireland. Tara is deeply rich in legend and folklore and is associated with goddess Meave ("The one who intoxicates' ') legend has it that any man who wished to establish himself as King of Tara would have to symbolically wed himself to her. Tara is also associated with many of the other pre Christian Gods of Ireland. As well as being a place of ancient Kings and Legends the Hill of Tara was also the setting for more recent drama of the key battles of Ireland 1798 Rebellion took place there with more than 4,000 united Irishmen making an unsuccessful stand against the British at the battle of Tara Hill. Over 350 rebels were killed, two memorials mark their memory a Celtic Cross and gravestone and the Lia Fáil. The Stone of Destiny was moved a short distance to mark their supposed burial place.

In 1843 Daniel "the Liberator" O'Connell drew on the symbolic power of Tara in the national consciousness to hold a monster rally to appeal Ireland's union with Britain attended by a crowd of over a million people.

Next to the statute of St.Patrick lies a church built in 1822 and is now used as a heritage centre. Inside the 19th Century Church there is the most amazing stained glass window to the east by artist Evie Hone. The window was commissioned in 1932 for the 1500th anniversary of the arrival of St. Patrick to Ireland. St. Patrick is said to have come to Tara to confront the ancient religion of pagans at its most powerful site.

On a clear day it is claimed that half the countries of Ireland can be seen from the top of Tara, even St. Brigid's shrine and Well Faughart in Co. Louth can be seen from Tara. Devoted to St. Brigid, one of Ireland's national patrons, the site is of ancient origin and would seem to have begun during her lifetime. Bridgid's cult grew to a status second only to that of Saint Patrick and to the Irish she was known as Mary of the Gael. According to tradition Brigid was born at Faughart, a few miles north of Dundalk about 450 AD. Brigid was one of the most remarkable women of her times and despite the numerous miracles attributed to her there is no doubt that her extraordinary spirituality, boundless charity and compassion for those in distress was real. She died at Kildare on February 1st. She is buried at Downpatrick with St. Columba and St. Patrick with whom she is patron Saint of Ireland. It is a tradition to make St Brigid's Crosses on her feast day February 1st and there are many rituals associated with the making of the crosses. It is traditionally believed that a St. Brigid's Cross protects the house from fire and evil. It is hung in many kitchens for this purpose.

In 1899 and 1902 a group calling themselves the British Israelites conducted a series of armature excavations at Rath na Seanadh (The Rath of Synods). They mistakenly believed the Ark of the Covenant was buried there and based on myths and legends connecting the Bible, Egypt and Ireland. In 1902 in a letter to the editor of the Irish Times, Tara was described by Douglas Hyde, George Moore and William Butler Yeats, key figures in the Gaelic Revival, as the "most consecrated spot in Ireland". Eventually the digs were stopped, but not before significant damage was done. These myths were probably designed by the early Irish Monks to draw connections between the Bible and the Prehistory of Ireland.

The Hill of Tara truly is the ancient soul of Ireland, the Stone age, Bronze Age, Iron Age people all were there.

It was here on the Hill of Tara that St. Patrick used the Shamrock to symbolise Ireland and explain Christianity to the High Kings using the 3 leaves and stem of the Shamrock. Each leaf represents the Father, the Son and the Holy Spirit and that's how he explained the Trinity, the concept of Christianity to the Pagan King. A theory that may predate the Hill of Tara's splendour before Milesian times is a legendary story naming the Hill of Tara as the Capital of the Tuatha De Danann the pre Milesian dwellers of Ireland.

When the Milesians established a seat in the Hill, the Hill became the place from which the Kings of Mide ruled Ireland or may have been all the northern half. The Tuath Dé Danann also known by the earlier name of Tuath Dé, tribe of Danu are a supernatural race in Irish mythology. They are thought to represent the main deities of pre-Christian Gaelic Ireland. The Tuatha Dé Danann constitute a pantheon whose attributes appeared in a number of forms throughout the Celtic World. The Tuath Dé dwell in the other world but interact with humans and the human world. They are associated with ancient passage tombs such as Brú na Bóinne, which were seen as portals to the other world. The Tuatha Dé Danann were descended from Nemed, leader of a precious wave of inhabitants of Ireland. They came from four mythical cities to the North of Ireland – Falias, Gorias, Murias and Finias – where they taught their skills in sciences, including architecture, the arts, and magic.

Much of what we know about the pre-christian peoples of Ireland comes from a series of early christian and medieval books the principal one being "Lebor Gabála Érenn", the book of invasions. Originally a collection of manuscripts painstakingly inscribed by monks of the seventh century as they recorded an oral tradition embracing five thousand years of history, its pages archived the arrivals and struggles of six different invaders as they landed on the green shores of Ireland giving us a unique glimpse into a dark age of our history.

The Tuatha Dé Danann were led to the underworld of Ireland by God of the Sea, Manannán shielded the defeated Tuatha Dé Danann from the eyes of the people of Ireland. They were surrounded by a great mist and over time, they became known as fairies of Ireland's folklore. There is little doubt that when the Tuatha Dé Danann arrived in Ireland they knew that it was previously the home of the Earth Goddess, for they were her people. They saw Ireland as a fertile ground where they could transplant their traditions and beliefs.

According to an ancient document known as the Annals of the Four Masters (Annála na gCeithre Maístrí compiled by Franciscan Monks between 1632-1636 from earlier texts), the Danann ruled from 1898

BC until 1700 BC, a short period indeed in which to have accumulated such fame. "The truth is not known, beneath the sky of stars, whether they were of heaven or earth".

In Ireland it is often said that every skilled man that had music and did enchantments secretly was of the Tuatha Dé Danann. Their reputation for practising magic and the arts as well as for being very intelligent, often cunning people, is ubiquitous across Ireland, as are references to their embodiment of a culture that emanated from the worship of the Earth Goddess. The Tuatha Dé Danann still tread the labyrinth of our temples and in the castles of their myths maintain their influence on Irish history, just as Irish history has maintained its influence over all of Europe. During the three thousand years following their epoch not a single event has been left uninformed by their rituals first introduced in the temple in the Hills of Kerry. The Dé Danann's sway over our religions and their ability to transmit thoughts and desires into the far future is a direct result of the systematic labour they put into building the Dingle Diamond standing just off the South Western shore of Ireland on Europe's most westerly point, the Dingle Peninsula. This is an area which generations of mystics, druids and monks have empathised with, all who have left monuments and myths as a testament to their beliefs. This area has one of the most concentrated assemblages of ancient structures in the World; tombs, temples, standing stones and early churches litter the countryside. The Dingle Diamond highlights the importance in the realm of the physical. Perhaps it was these magical people The Tuatha Dé Danann, half God like beings, half alien created the Dingle Diamond. History records what happened to the Tuatha Dé Danann and their mission. Their legacy to this day is woven into our consciousness.

The name Tara originates as an Irish Gaelic and Sanskrit name Tara means "elevated place" in Gaelic and "Star" in Sanskrit. Tara is a girl's name. Ancient Tara was the site on the "Stone of Destiny" on which

Irish Kings resided. In Hindu mythology, Tara is one of the names of the wife of Lord Shiva. In America Tara is commonly used as a baby name meaning Goddess of the Sea. In Margaret Mitchell's Novel, Gone with the Wind, and a subsequent film made later, The name 'Tara' was the name given to the family plantation. Some sources also suggest Tara is a diminutive of Tamara.

Who was the Goddess Tara? Tara is worshipped in both Hinduism and Buddhism as the Goddess of Compassion and protection. In Hinduism she is a form of the female energy known as Shakti. The name comes from the Sanskrit Root tar, meaning "protection". In other Indian languages the name translates as "Star".

Tara first appeared as a deity in Hinduism, but was later adopted by Buddhism. In fact, in some traditions she is considered the female Buddha. In Tibetan Buddhism she is the most popular deity worshipped. Tara is the second of the ten great wisdom Goddesses. In tantric traditions, she may be considered an incarnation of Durga, Paravati or Mahadevi, Goddess Tara protects those on their journey to enlightenment as well as earthly travellers. In some traditions Tara appears in different forms; the two best known versions of her are White Tara, the embodiment of compassion and peace, and Green Tara who is the great protector and caretaker of observations.

Two of the Yoga poses that honour the Goddess Tara are Star Pose (Tara Sana) and seated Tara. In Star pose, the Yogi sits in butterfly pose, grasps the feet and folds forward. In seated Tara, one leg is bent with the shin on the ground and close to the body while the other leg is being with the knee pointing to the sky and the sole of the foot on the ground. BhumiSparsha Mudra is recommended with the corresponding hand resting on the ground next to the soled foot and the other hand covering the heart centre. The following are Mantras dedicated to Goddess Tara.

Tara Mantra

Om Hreem Treem Hum Phat

This is the Five word Panchakshara Tara Mantra to Goddess Tara.
This mantra will give you willpower & strength and will help you
connect to Divine Mother Energy.

Tara Gayatri Mantra

Om Tarayae ch vidhmahe mahograyae ch dhimahi tanno devi prachodayat

This mantra will make you so strong that you can experience
Mother Love & Divine Bliss.

The Hill of Tara was included in the World monuments funds 2008 watch list of the 100 most endangered sites in the World. It was included in 2009, in the 15 most endangered cultural treasures in the World by the Smithsonian institution.

While visiting Tara I lay on the grass and meditated. I connected with many new angels and saints. I reconnected with St. Patrick, whose first vision appeared to me on the sacred site of ArchAngel Michael's Well in Ballinskelligs, Co.Kerry which is part of the Dingle Diamond, at the start of my journey with the Discovery of Kingdom Water. The Hill of Tara truly is the Irish Valley of Angels.

"The pilgrim route is for those who are good; it is the lack of vices, the thwarting of the body, the increase of virtues, pardon for sins, sorrow for the penitent, the road of the righteous, love of the saints, faith in the resurrection and the reward of the blessed, a separation from hell, the protection of the heavens.

The Codes Calistinus, an 1173 anthology for pilgrims to Compostela. When I visited the Valley of Flowers in the Himalayas for me the biggest reason to love and remember the trek is the beautiful Valley itself. When you stand at the entry of the Valley you see ahead of you a colourful carpet laid out. The Valley is an area of 87 sq. kilometres wide and more than 10 kilometres long. It is deep in the heart of the Himalayas, a mountain side meadow at an altitude of 11,500 feet (3,500 metres) with over 1000 varieties of flowers, shrubs, orchids and other plants carpeting the Valley.

The Valley of Flowers is a naturalist's heaven and a trekkers delight. With a stunning backdrop of the mighty Himalayan ranges discovered in 1931, when three British mountaineers led by Frank S. Smythe lost their way and chanced upon this spectacular Valley. While trekking through this Valley you truly are at the highest state, yet you are down and hold the strongest attachment with our Mother Earth. You truly are ego-less in this Valley of Flowers.

I was witnessing all the drama of my life, forgiving always no matter what and kept showering my blessings with the great treasure of nature and for the survival of life on this heavenly planet of earth. In this Valley of Flowers along the Valley I sat and meditated completely detached and completely one with the Universe. The eye catching vision of the exotic flowers like marigolds, daisies and anemones were something to behold. It is no wonder this Valley is also home to such rare and amazing species like the Gray Langur, the flying squirrel, the Himalayan weasel, the red fox and the black bear and the lime butterfly.

No words can prepare you for the beauty of this Valley. The whole area has a feeling of love, peace and calming feel that would warm anyone's soul. It is hard to describe, but it kind of feels like your heart wants your entire body and the soul with the heat of an internal flame to shower you with warm blessings. Even our souls speak a language that is beyond human understanding. I felt a deep connection with this Valley so rare that at one stage I thought the universe would not let us part. It is no wonder that this Valley of Flowers is where Angels romance and experience divine love. This Valley of Flowers attracts Angels into your love life. They give you more clarity about soul-mate relationships, healing from the past and help you attract more love into your life.

Angels meet each other here and experience divine love while divine love can be called perfect, infinite, enduring and universal it can not correctly be characterized as unconditional. The angels love for each other is divine by definition. Scriptures also describe it as perfect. It is infinite because the atonement was an act of love for all the angels who ever lived, who now live, and who will ever live. It is also infinite because it transcends time but is conditional because God loves us all and wants us to be happy. The full flower love of Valley of Flowers is the full flower of divine love and our greatest blessings from that love are conditional where the angels enjoy the blessings and rejoice forever in the Valley of Flowers.

For countless centuries distant shrines have beckoned. The urge to demonstrate devotion, to seek meaning in sacred places, to step away from routines to pursue a deeper purpose, persists despite the advent of jet travel, digital technology and global communication networks. One thing for sure, regardless of religion, all these divine places from Gyanganj to The Hill of Tara, the Dingle Diamond to Devprayag, to the Valley of flowers these are all places where angels intermingle and meet and worship and still perform rituals on these natural sacred sites which were constructed for ritualistic purposes. The craving to visit these sacred sites no doubt will stir the souls of generations to come.

Chapter 11

Prayers & Meditation

Every religion believes in Angels. They pray to their Angels and in return they receive divine power. Creating positive energy on a daily basis by attracting and connecting with your angels through prayer and meditation can transform your life. The most important way to discipline the mind, and thus connect with Truth, is to spend regular time in prayer and meditation. Prayer can make a tremendous difference in life. If we all applied ourselves to prayer, we could free ourselves from many of the ills of humanity.

Prayer is man's steady effort to know God, Nature and the Supreme. When we pray, we use prayer as an exercise to change our thought habits and our living habits so that we may set up a new and better activity in accord with the divine law, rather than with the suggestions we have received from various external sources. Prayer accomplishes many things. It develops our character to its highest state. It builds a mind that is always open to spirit. We attain a oneness with God.

When we sit and meditate, we become receptacles, or Holy Grails, to be filled with the Divine mind. We are inspired with fresh resolve, with new creative thought, with solutions to our problems, and with the understanding of Truth that we need. We get the most vivid revelations when in a meditative state of mind. This proves that we have a divine purpose. God purposely created you to know, love, and worship him. God is not hiding in the church or temple. God is reflected everywhere and in everything.

Prayer is the bridge that enables you to speak and connect to angels. It is the medium of miracles that allows you to send your thoughts, thanks and intentions to heaven. Prayer is our conversation with our guardians. It is the moment we choose to connect. I believe that when we pray, we create an altar in our minds where we can commune with the Divine. We raise our vibes and draw the golden light of the angels towards us like a magnet.

Prayer is speaking to heaven. It is an open call, like a conference call to heaven. God, the angels and our ascended masters, spirit guides and ancestors are up there waiting for our call and they begin to hear our thoughts and our requests. It is through prayer that we can ask for help; it is through prayer that we open up to their help. Prayer and meditation energy help to build values and pure hearts. It is through my own daily prayer and meditation practice that I have discovered the true power of the angels.

Like snowflakes, we all come in different shapes, with a unique mission on Earth. No matter what your calling is, this world is depending on you. Existence is a puzzle; without you in it, it would be incomplete. Prayer can help you achieve and overcome anything. God has been waiting for you. He has always been right here, closer than your jugular vein, closer than the breath in your lungs, closer than the words on your tongue. God is here with you. Return to Him. Return to his ocean of love and let him embrace you along with all the angels with the healing waves of his endless mercy.

Prayers to activate your angels

Angels are always everywhere around you. They are watching over you and leaving signs of their presence in your daily life. Have you actively reached out to try and connect with your angels? You need to ask them to help and guide you. Use this gift box of prayers to activate your angels, and bring their heavenly guidance and assistance into your life.

Prayer to your Guardian Angel of God

Angel of God, my guardian dear,
to whom God's love commits me here,
ever this day (or night) be at my side,
to light, to guard, to rule and guide.
Amen

The Beatitudes

Blest are the poor in spirit: the reign of God is theirs.
Blest are the sorrowing: they shall be consoled.
Blest are the lowly: they shall inherit the land.
Blest are they who hunger and thirst for holiness: they shall have their fill.
Blest are they who show mercy: mercy shall be theirs.
Blest are the single-hearted, for they shall see God.
Blest are the peacemakers: they shall be called sons of God.
Blest are those persecuted for holiness' sake: the reign of God is theirs.
Mt. 5:3:10

Saint Faustina's Healing Prayer

"Jesus may Your pure and healthy blood circulate in my poor ailing organism, and may Your pure and healthy body transform my weak unhealthy body, and may a healthy and vigorous life flow once again within me, if it is truly Your Holy Will.
Amen

Prayer for Forgiveness

Heavenly Father, thank You that You are quick to forgive. Thank You, that You have removed our sins as far as the east is from the west. Right now, Lord, we ask of You mercy and compassion, and we implore the forgiveness of sins. In Jesus' name.
Amen

Prayer for Forgiveness for my Enemy

Loving Father, thank You for the example of Jesus Who cried, Father forgive on the cross. Help me to be one that freely and willingly prays forgiveness over those who are my enemies, and those who, for whatever reason, dislike or try to harm me.

Lord, I thank You that even the people in our lives who despise and i'll-use us have a divine purpose in Your perfect plan, in that it drives us back into Your arms of love. From here, we can lift them up to Your throne of grace in prayer, asking for their forgiveness and salvation and releasing in us any pent-up hatred or bitterness that is so damaging to our souls and well-being.

*Forgive my enemies, Lord, and all those who have tried to hurt or harm
me. Look down in pity on all those who I term 'enemies' and give me the
grace to show them the love of Christ in my actions and attitudes towards
them. Keep my thoughts from becoming resentful or seeking revenge, but
rather release in my heart the peace that only comes from casting all my
cares on You, including my enemies.*

*Give me the grace, not only to truly forgive all my enemies but also to
bless those who persecute me, for in so doing I see a dim reflection of Your
enormous grace towards me, for which I praise and thank You. In Jesus'
blessed name,*

Amen

PRAYERS TO THE SACRED HEART

Come to me, all you who labour and are ever-burdened,
and I will give you rest.
Shoulder my yoke and learn from me,
for I am gentle and humble in heart,
and you will find rest for your souls.
Yes, my yoke is easy and my burden is light.
Matthew. 11.

Prayer for Peace and Tranquillity

Let nothing ever disturb you,
Nothing affright you;
All things are passing,
God never changes.
Patient endurance
Attains to all things;
Who God possesses

In nothing is wanting:
Alone God suffices.
Amen
St. Teresa of Avila

Prayers for Guidance

May God, the Lord, bless us and make us perfect and holy in his sight.
May the riches of his glory abound in us.
May he instruct us with the word of truth,
inform us with the gospel of salvation,
and enrich us with his love;
thorough Christ our Lord.
Amen

Prayer for Survivors and Victims of Sexual Abuse

Dear God,
Loving God, I know that you hold me in the palm of your hand.
I know it is so. But why, O Lord, why?

I rage at this sin against me, at this defilement of my body,
this assault on my peace of mind.

I mourn my lost serenity, security, confidence;
I mourn the loss of my ease and open nature.
I hate what this assault has done to me.
I feel that my body and soul may never be the same.

What has been forced upon me may not be forgotten.
But send your healing upon me like cool rain.

Soothe my spirit with the balm of your tender love.
Help me to feel secure again, as safe as ever within the shelter of the Lord.

Let my anger not turn inward to self-loathing,
but outward for action and purpose: to help others like me,
to bring hope to those whose faith is not so strong.
Help me, with your grace,
to move beyond the victim, to call myself survivor instead.

May you forgive this man's offence against me,
and grant me the peace and serenity
of a mind and body made whole again.
Amen

Short Morning Prayer to your Guardian Angel

Angel of God,
my holy protector,
given to me from heaven by God for my protection,
I fervently beseech you:
enlighten me and preserve me from all evil,
instruct me in good deeds and direct me on the path of salvation.
Amen

Prayer to St. Nicholas For a Sick Child

Saint Nicholas, who like the Saviour,
loved children so tenderly and gave generously to those in need,
listen to us who plead for this sick child
who is so dear to our hearts.

We thank God for the great gift of our child
and we pray that He relieve this child of pain
and free him/her from suffering.
Obtain strength when he/she is weary,
hope when discouraged,
and joy when downhearted.
May the Lord, through your intercession,
restore perfect health if such be His divine will.
Amen

A Prayer to The Ivory Swan Goddess – Kuan Yin

Beloved Kuan Yin, Mother of Peace, Beauty and Compassion, the Light
In you is the same Light in me! Help me to be at peace with my eternal
innocence and purity. Ivory Swan Goddess, please help me let go of old
beliefs and experiences of shame, self-condemnation or judgment that no
longer serve me. I now honour and accept wholly and completely that the
Light in you is the same Divine Light in Me. Om Mane Padme Hum

A Prayer for Clairvoyance

Thank you, dear angels, for awakening my sight
So I can clearly see and sense you.
I allow you to open my energy so I can perceive
Nothing but the truth and the loving energy that surrounds me.

I align myself with love and peace and allow my energy
to be raised to yours!
I am pleased and blessed to see you, and my eyes are open.

And so it is!
Amen

Healing Prayer

Lord God,
In the face of illness, we recognise our need.
We need strength, we need peace, and we need You.
Just as Jesus healed those who came to him,
Extend your hand so that (name) will receive your healing power.
I ask this with my whole heart, with trust in You.
Amen

Prayer for Happiness and Joy

Dear Lord,
Thank you for all your blessings,
For my family, friends and neighbours.
Thank you for all the beauty
In the skies, the lakes and the mountains.
Thank you for all the excitement of celebration,
Birthdays, weddings and christenings.
Thank you for all the variety of animals, birds
And insects.
Thank you for all the enrichment of music, art
And literature.
Thank you for the amazing jigsaw of life!
What a beautiful picture is made when I place all these pieces together!
Thank you for the promise of eternity,
For the sacrifices you made so that I can be free,
Free to make my life into a glorious patchwork of thanksgiving
That carries me onwards to the promises of new heavenly pieces
to add to all that I already hold.
Thank you.
Amen

Memorare Prayer

The Memorare, invites us to ask the Blessed Mother for her assistance and her grace especially when we feel most troubled in our daily lives.

REMEMBER, O most gracious Virgin Mary, that never was it known that anyone who fled to thy protection, implored thy help, or sought thy intercession was left unaided. Inspired with this confidence, I fly to thee, O Virgin of virgins, my Mother; to thee do I come; before thee I stand, sinful and sorrowful. O Mother of the Word Incarnate, despise not my petitions, but in thy mercy hear and answer me.
Amen

The Jesus Prayer

(Repeat this prayer as many times as possible regularly during the day)

Lord Jesus Christ, Son of God, have mercy on me as a sinner.
Amen

Prayer to Mary Queen of Angels

August Queen of Heaven!

Sovereign Mistress of the angels!

You who from the beginning as received from God the power and mission to crush the head of Satan,

we humbly beseech you to send your Legions, that, under your command and by your power,

they may pursue the evil spirits,
encountered them on every side,
resist their bold attacks and drive them into the
abyss of eternal woe.
Amen

Prayer for Protection and Salvation

Saint Michael the Archangel, helps us against the evils which threaten the Salvation of our souls.

Guide us to build up our spiritual Life, and assist us with the means of obtaining Graces, Virtues, Gifts of the Holy Spirit and the Sacraments, which keep us in a Holy State at all times.

Saint Michael, place your sword at my door; at the foot of my bed; in front of my car when I drive and by my side when I walk and guard and protect me against all evil and all temptation.

Amen

Prayer to Be Freed From My Burdensome Addiction

Dear Lord Jesus, my addiction is a terrible burden and such a shame to me and yet I find myself constantly returning to behaviours that I hate and long to be able to shed. I am so ashamed Lord, and yet I know that You were the One Who said that You came to set the captives free, and Lord I am a captive. I am a captive and slave of this terrible addiction and yet too long to be freed and to live a normal life.

Free me Lord I pray from this compulsion, for it is stifling my life and has cost me many dear friends as well as my job. I long to be free to live as I ought.

I have heard the gospel and I do believe that Jesus died to take the full punishment for all my sins, including my addiction and I believe that He rose the third day, which broke the power of death in the lives of all who believe. So I am coming to you to ask You Lord to give me the abundant life that You have promised. I know that eternal life is now my portion, but I pray that I may be free of my addiction in this life so that I may serve You as You deserve. I ask this in the name of the Lord Jesus,

Amen

Prayer for Babies in the Womb

Heavenly Father, I bring before You all women that are pregnant, and all couples that are expecting a little baby to be born into their home. I ask for your protection for all babies that are secretly being formed in the womb of their mother.
Amen

Prayer to the Celestial Mountain

Beloved Kuan Yin, in the Ashram of your Celestial Mountain, hear me, please help me to let go of my difficulties in receiving help, in any feelings of worthlessness or distrust that prevent me from being guided, moved and placed in positions of divine assistance for my greatest good. Help me feel worthy of help and help me receive that help which comes to me in unconditional love now. Thank you!
Om Mani Padme Hum

A Broken Relationship

How can I face the future Lord, for my heart is broken. The love of my life has grown weary of our relationship and has walked away from me and I am heart-broken Lord.

Why did this have to happen? I thought that You had brought us together. I thought that our love for each other had been made in heaven. But now they have gone and my heart is broken.

I pray that You will help me to face what has happened and not to hanker for something that might have been. Help me to look forward to the future and not regret the past. And today Lord- now, I put my trust in You for I want You to guide my path, for I know that when I follow my own heart it always ends in distress.

Lead me Lord. Lead me in the way that I should go. Heal my fractured heart and I pray that instead of bitterness being the fruit of this experience, that You will bring beauty for brokenness and replace despair with Your joy. Your hand I commit my life, my future, my relationship, and myself.

Draw me ever closer into secure communion with Yourself. Thank You that You really do wipe away every tear from our eyes. I love You Lord.
Amen

Fatima Prayer

O Jesus, forgive us our sins
save us from the fire of hell.
Lead all souls to Heaven,
especially those most in need of your mercy.
Amen

The Hail Mary

Hail, Mary, full of grace, the lord is with thee. Blessed art thou amongst women and blessed is the fruit of thy womb Jesus. Holy Mary Mother of God, Pray for our sinners, now and at the hour of our death.
Amen

Prayer to Mother Teresa

Mother Theresa prayed this inspirational prayer on a daily basis; the prayer sums up her spirituality and desire to spread Jesus's love everywhere she went.

Dear Jesus, help me to spread thy fragrance everywhere I go.
Flood my soul with thy spirit and love.
Penetrate and possess my whole being so utterly that all my life may only be a radiance of thine.
Shine through me and be so in me that every soul I come in contact with may feel thy presence in my soul.
Let them look and see no longer me but only Jesus.
Stay with me and then I shall begin to shine as you shine, so to shine as to be the light to others.
Amen

Prayer of Light

Oh Allah!
Place light in my heart
And light in my tongue
And light in my hearing
And light in my seeing
And light form above me
And light from below me
And light on my right
And light on my left
And light ahead of me
And light behind me
Place light in my Soul
Magnify for me light
And amplify for me light
Oh Allah! Grant me light
And place light in my nerves
And light in my blood
And light in my body
And light in my hair
And light in my skin
Increase me in light
Increase me in light
Grant me light upon light!

— Prophet Muhammad

Meditation Mantras

Meditation is not a religion, but all the great world religions have the same conclusive principle - the ultimate goal of man is to become one with the Divine. This is interpreted in different ways by different religions but all agree that this union with the Divine can only be achieved through meditation.

Tool box guide to meditation

The best times to meditate are sunrise & sunset
Invest in a set of 108 Mala Prayer beads
Sit in a comfortable position with your spine straight
Find the best Mantra to suit your intention
Get comfortable & set your intention
Focus on your breathing
Chant OM OM OM
Start chanting your mantra and focus on the sound of the mantra
Continue chanting the mantra for as long as you like.
Finish with OM OM OM.
Namaste and Amen

OM OM OM

Chanting Om or Aum is a sacred practice that helps our mind and body to energize. OM is considered sacred in Hinduism, Buddhism, Sikhism and Jainism. It is the first sound of the universe. Om connects all living beings to nature and the universe.

Om Namah Shivaya

This is one of the most powerful Hindu Mantras. It means 'The Inner Self'. It's said that regular practice of this mantra will bring you very close to the divine inner nature within all of us.

Gayatri Mantra
Om Bhur Bhuva Swaha tat savitur varenyam bhargo devasya dhimahi dhiyo yo nah prachodayat.

The Gayatri Mantra is considered to be the mother mantra of all mantras, the most powerful Vedic mantra. It has immense power, can be sung at any time and at any place, and redeems whoever sings it. It is directly addressed to our Divine Mother, Love and reverence for the mantra and faith in the results, promises much more important than mere mechanical repetition while the mind wanders off in other subjects.

Om Mani Padme Hum
Praise to the jewel in the lotus. This is the most commonly chanted mantra in Yoga. Its essence is both pure and powerful.

Mantra for the Nine Planets
All planets control the world. These nine mantras are very powerful and they can help invite the blessings of the nine planets for the benefit of you chanting these mantras
Om Suraya Namaha - Sun
Om Chandraya Namaha - Moon
Om Mangalai Namaha - Mars
Om Budhaya Namaha - Mercury
OM Brihas Pathaye Namaha - Jupiter

Om Shukra-Ya Namaha - Venus
Om Shani Devaya Namaha - Saturn
Om Rahuve Namaha - Dragons Head
Om Ketave Namah - Dragon's Tail

Om Hleem Namaha

This Mantra is associated with Hindu Wisdom Goddess Bagalamukhi, to protect you from your enemies.

Om Aim Namaha

This Mantra invokes Goddess Saraswati, for wisdom, success and knowledge. It calms your mind and relaxes you too.

Om Shreem Namaha

This mantra is to attain power and wealth from Goddess Mahalakshmi.

Om Hreem Hamsa Soham Swaha

This mantra is recited for Kundalini Awakening within the Goddess.

Al - Mutakabbir Namaha

This is a Sufi mantra meaning the Greatest. For the Sufi the relationship to God is that of lover; Sufis are known as the lovers of God.

Om Tare Tuttare Ture Swaha

This is a Buddhist mantra and means 'I prostrate to the liberator, mother of all the vicious ones'.

Om Hreem Sankatey Mam Rogam Nasaaya Swaaha

This mantra is for the blessing of good health.

Om Namo Narayana Namaha

This is Lord Vishnu's mantra of peace, it removes negative emotions like ego, and anger. It clears obstacles and distractions and generates Harmony.

Om Kreem Kali Kayai Namaha

Kali is the Hindu Goddess who removes the ego and liberates the soul from the cycle of birth and death. This mantra will protect one from all the evil forces. Kali is the Goddess of Transformation.

Mrityunjaya Mantra

Om Tri-Yum-Ba-Kum Yajamahey, Sugandhim pushti vardhanam, Uur-Vaa Rukavima Bandhanan, Meth-Yor Mokshe - Ya Ma'am-R-Thaath.

The benefits of chanting this mantra is to surround yourself with the protection of Lord Shiva's energy, which is the most powerful energy.

Om Yastu Namaha

This mantra removes from your all home negative energy and negative thoughts.

Ya Noor Ya Hafiz

This mantra is for your protection.

Ya latif Ya latif Ya latif Ya latif

Allah will grant abundance and solve problems while chanting this mantra.

Om Gam Gung Ganapataye Namaha

This mantra is for Hindu God Lord Ganapati. Reciting this mantra gives the Devotees wisdom, power, knowledge, fortune, happiness and divine protection by chanting this regularly.

Shani Gayatri Mantra

Om Shanaischaraya vidhmahe Surya Putraya dhimahi tanno surya prachodayat

Shani is embodied in the planet saturn and is the lord of saturday, he is the chief justice of the world, he is known as the greatest teacher and well - wisher for the righteous, he is the protector of property.

Tara Mantra

Om Hreem Treem Hum Phat

This is the Five word Panchakshara Tara Mantra to Goddess Tara. This mantra will give you willpower & strength and will help you connect to Divine Mother Energy.

Tara Gayatri Mantra

Om Tarayae Ch Vidhmahe Mahograyae ch dhimahi tanno devi Prachodayat

This mantra will make you so strong that you can experience Mother Love & Divine Bliss.

On my journey to release, understand and utilise Kingdom Water, I learned so much that I never expected to know. I learned about water's chemical composition, about drilling techniques and bottling systems. But I also learned about angles, Divine will, Divine presence, the beauty and love of our ancestors and guardians. About harnessing the energy of the earth and bringing angelic presences into our daily lives to enhance and beautify these lives. I learned these things in Ireland, in France, in Italy and in India, more than I ever expected to know, and because of what I learned, I now see my own life and the world around me differently.

With this book I have chosen to share some of what I learned, in the hopes that you too will start to recognise the presence of the angelic and the Divine in your own life.

I suppose the fundamental message of my book was to tell my spiritual journey, my true story as it actually happened. On this journey I have realized powers in myself that at first, I could never have imagined. I have the ability now to see the happenings of the future. God gives this wisdom and knowledge to very few people. Only those who have had a kundalini awakening can experience what I have experienced. When a kundalini awakens in a person, the chakras awake. Only then can you see the future and connect with God and attain self-knowledge. Never in my wildest dreams did I ever think I would experience a Kundalini Awakening or publish two books, and now I want this to inspire other people to believe that if you have faith and practice, you too could experience these things.

I am an ordinary businesswoman, mother of two children. I never asked for any of this to happen to me. It is through the deep faith in my heart that all this has happened. I want this book to enrich and enlighten people, to let them see that there are greater forces at work. I want people who have written great books and never published them to be inspired to self-publish their stories.

For me the biggest message of all is that hard work always pays off, and to never ever give up; to follow your dreams. For all that this journey has brought me now, I look back and say to myself 'why me? Why was I chosen?' Then I pinch myself and say, 'why not you Michelle Keane?' Because I wouldn't change a thing. Not for all the tea in China.

So thank you God and Our Lady, my ancestors, ascended masters, saints and spirit guides. It is only through your grace and divine mercy that I have made it this far.

Namaste and Amen.

Acknowledgements

My angels along the way

As with everything I have done in my life, this book would not have been possible without the love and support of many people.

I would not be who I am today without the steady hand and unconditional love of my mother Thérèse. She has always been my rock, allowing me the freedom to be who I am, while never allowing my feet to get too far off the ground. My father Luke, who gave me this beautiful gift of writing.

Thank you to all the amazing friends in my life who have kept me lifted up. You know who you are and what you mean to me: my girlfriends, my mentors, my spiritual teachers; all of you have supported me during this writing process and have helped me become a better woman. They are my soul mates on this life's journey and many other life times as well. My supreme joy is knowing that we will always be together, to the very end of time.

My heartfelt and enduring thanks go to my Indian Guruji, Shashi Dubey, whose expertise and support contributed mightily to this book. He is a true friend.

I thank the Angels who told me that I had to write this book and publish it myself. At every stage I have been divinely guided in writing this manuscript. I would like to express my love and gratitude to all my angels, spirit guides, guardian angels, archangels, ancestors, saints and ascended masters. Without their guidance, this book would not have come into existence. To my spiritual teachers and to the greatest guru of all life.

Giving birth to this book has been one of the most challenging experiences I have faced. The angels forced me to search my soul, revisit old wounds, be aware of where I am in my life and bring these stories from my soul onto paper, to help people throughout the world connect with their own angels.

To those who serve as angels in heaven and upon the earth. Special thanks to my ancestors and Archangel Michael for giving me Kingdom Water, and to my angels for guiding me every step of the way on my journey of discovery.

I am so privileged to have been born and raised in the Kingdom of Kerry. Knocknagoshel means far more to me than just another townland in Kerry. It is where my roots are, and where my ancestors thrived.

I want to send gratitude to God, Our Lady, Mother Nature, my ancestors, all the saints, ascended masters, my spirit guides and to the thousands of angels that have guided me to write *Kingdom of Angels*. It is through the deep faith in my soul that you have rewarded me with so much. For that I divinely salute you and thank you. Namaste and Amen.

"Arise Knocknagoshel and take your place among the nations of the earth".
Charles Stuart Parnell - 1891

Praise for *Kingdom of Angels*

"As an author, Michelle Keane is the master of two very different skills; expert scholarship and an easy engaging style.

This book *Kingdom of Angels*, is the inner wisdom and bliss of angels within Michelle, she has a spiritual gift that lets us experience Angels, Saints & Ascended Masters in a way that no longer appears to be far beyond you.

Her Book is a passport into the spiritual realm of these special friends of God."

Dr. Ashwani Chopra,
M.B.B.S. M.D. (DELHI) M.R.C.P. (LONDON),
Consultant Physician Gastroenterologist,
Director AASHLOK Hospital,
New Delhi,
India.